GCSE AQA
Physics
The Workbook

This book is for anyone doing **GCSE AQA Physics**.

It's full of **tricky questions**... each one designed to make you **sweat** — because that's the only way you'll get any **better**.

There are questions to see **what facts** you know. There are questions to see how well you can **apply those facts**. And there are questions to see what you know about **how science works**.

It's also got some daft bits in to try and make the whole experience at least vaguely entertaining for you.

What CGP is all about

Our sole aim here at CGP is to produce the highest quality books — carefully written, immaculately presented and dangerously close to being funny.

Then we work our socks off to get them out to you — at the cheapest possible prices.

Contents

PHYSICS 2B — ELECTRICITY AND THE ATOM

PHYSICS 3A — MEDICAL APPLICATIONS OF PHYSICS

PHYSICS 3B — FORCES AND ELECTROMAGNETISM

Published by CGP

Editors:
Helena Hayes, Felicity Inkpen, Julie Wakeling, Sarah Williams.

Contributors:
Steve Coggins, Paddy Gannon, Dr Giles R Greenway, Frederick Langridge,
Barbara Mascetti, John Myers.

ISBN: 978 1 84762 628 8

With thanks to Michael Birch, Mark A Edwards, David Ryan, Karen Wells and Dawn Wright
for the proofreading.

Pages 27, 34, 98 and 99 contain public sector information published by the Health and Safety
Executive and licensed under the Open Government Licence v1.0.

Groovy website: www.cgpbooks.co.uk

Printed by Elanders Ltd, Newcastle upon Tyne.
Jolly bits of clipart from CorelDRAW®

Based on the classic CGP style created by Richard Parsons.

Heat Radiation

Q1 a) Tick the correct boxes to show whether each of the following statements is true or false.

True   False

i) Heat energy can be transferred by radiation, conduction and convection. ☐ ☐

ii) Conduction involves the transfer of energy between moving particles. ☐ ☐

iii) Hot objects do not absorb infrared radiation. ☐ ☐

iv) Convection always involves a moving liquid or gas. ☐ ☐

v) Cold objects do not emit infrared radiation. ☐ ☐

b) Write out corrected versions of the **false** statements.

....

....

Q2 Complete the following sentences by circling the correct words.

a) Dark, matt surfaces are **good** / **poor** absorbers and **good** / **poor** emitters of infrared radiation.

b) The best surfaces for radiating infrared are **good** / **poor** absorbers and **good** / **poor** emitters.

c) Silvered surfaces are **good** / **poor** absorbers and **good** / **poor** emitters of infrared radiation.

d) The best surfaces for solar hot water panels are **good** / **poor** absorbers and **good** / **poor** emitters.

Q3 Each sentence below contains two mistakes. Write out a correct version of each.

a) Infrared radiation is emitted from the centre of hot solid objects, but not from liquids or gases.

....

....

b) Only some objects absorb infrared radiation — the bigger the difference in temperature between an object and its surroundings, the slower the rate of heat transfer.

....

....

Q4 Give a scientific reason why steel **electric kettles** are often made very **shiny**.

....

....

2

Heat Radiation

Q5 Tick the correct boxes below to show whether the sentences are true or false.

True False

a) The amount of infrared radiation absorbed by a surface depends only on its colour. ☐ ☐

b) The hotter a surface is, the more infrared radiation it radiates. ☐ ☐

c) Good absorbers of infrared radiation are also good emitters of infrared radiation. ☐ ☐

d) White glossy surfaces absorb infrared radiation better than dark matt surfaces. ☐ ☐

e) Some solar panels are designed to absorb radiation from the Sun to heat water for washing or heating a building. ☐ ☐

Q6 Three flasks, each containing 100 ml of water, are placed in closed boxes. The water in the flasks and the air in the boxes are at different temperatures, as shown.

A Air in box 55°C Water 60°C

B Air in box 50°C Water 65°C

C Air in box 65°C Water 70°C

Which flask will cool fastest? Give a reason for your answer.

Flask .... will cool fastest because ....

....

....

Q7 Mr Green makes a **solar hot water panel** from an old white central heating radiator made of **steel**.

wooden support
old radiator
wooden roof
air space
pipes connected to hot water tank and pump

Mr Green fixes the panel to the roof of his garden shed. Sadly, he finds that the water does not get very hot, even on sunny days.

Explain how Mr Green could improve the design of his solar hot water panel.

....

....

....

....

Physics 1a — Energy

Kinetic Theory

Q1 The pictures below show the arrangement of particles in a solid, a liquid and a gas.
Draw lines to match each picture and description to the correct word.

GAS

LIQUID

SOLID

There are weak forces of attraction between the particles.

There are almost no forces of attraction between the particles.

There are strong forces of attraction holding the particles close together.

Q2 Tick the correct boxes below to show whether the sentences are true or false.

True False

a) The particles in a **liquid** are free to move at **high** speeds. ☐ ☐

b) The particles in a gas have **more** energy than those in liquids and solids. ☐ ☐

c) In a solid, the particles can only **vibrate** about a fixed position. ☐ ☐

d) In a liquid, the particles form **irregular** arrangements. ☐ ☐

e) The particles in a liquid have **less** energy than those in a solid. ☐ ☐

Q3 If you keep heating a solid, it will eventually melt and turn into a liquid. Explain why this happens, in terms of particles.

....

....

....

....

....

Conduction

Q1 Tick to show whether the sentences below are true or false.

True False

a) Conduction involves **energy** passing between **vibrating particles**. ☐ ☐

b) Some **metals** are very **poor** conductors. ☐ ☐

c) **Solids** are usually better **conductors** of heat than liquids and gases. ☐ ☐

d) **Conduction** is usually **faster** in **denser solids**. ☐ ☐

Q2 George picks up a piece of wood and a metal spoon. Both have the same temperature: 20 °C.

Explain why the metal spoon feels **colder** to the touch than the piece of wood.

....

....

Q3 For each of the descriptions below, say whether it describes an **insulator** or a **conductor**.

a) There are **large** spaces between the particles. ....

b) Heat transfer is **quick** because the particles in the material **collide** a lot. ....

c) Some types of these materials contain **free electrons**. ....

d) The particles are **close** together. ....

Q4 Sajid, Mamphela and Ruth are discussing why copper is a good conductor of heat.

Sajid says, **"Copper is a great conductor because it's got electrons in it."**

Mamphela says, **"It conducts well because it's shiny."**

Ruth says, **"It conducts well because all its particles have kinetic energy."**

Each pupil has made at least one mistake. Explain one mistake made by:

a) Sajid ....

....

b) Mamphela ....

....

c) Ruth ....

....

Convection

Q1 a) Tick the boxes next to the sentences to show whether they are true or false.

                                                                True False

    i) In a hot water tank, an immersion heater is usually placed at the bottom of the tank. ☐ ☐

    ii) The hotter the water, the denser it is. ☐ ☐

    iii) Convection currents happen when hot water displaces cold water. ☐ ☐

    iv) Convection currents can happen in water but not in air. ☐ ☐

b) Write a correction for each false sentence.

....

....

....

Q2 Match each observation with an explanation.

The very bottom of a hot water tank stays cold...

Warm air rises...

A small heater can send heat all over a room...

because water doesn't conduct much heat.

because heat flows from warm places to cooler ones.

because it is not so dense.

Q3 The picture below shows a radiator being used to heat up a room.

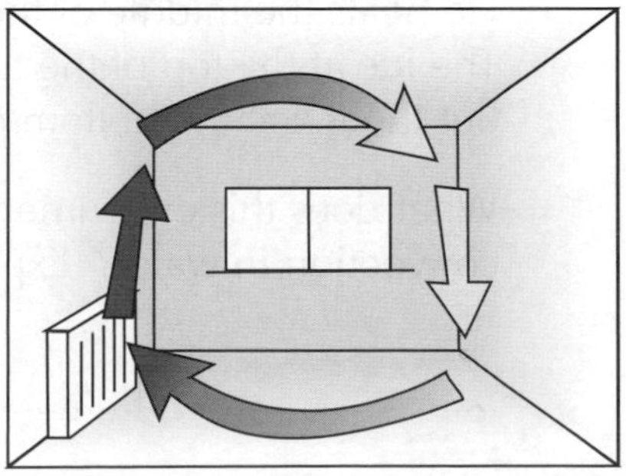

a) What happens to the **energy** of the particles in the air next to the radiator? Explain your answer.

....

....

....

b) Briefly explain how the change in the particles' energy causes a convection current in the room.

....

....

....

<u>Convection</u>

Q4   Convection can make water flow round the pipes in a house, without using a pump.
Miss Jenkins demonstrates this to her pupils using the apparatus below.

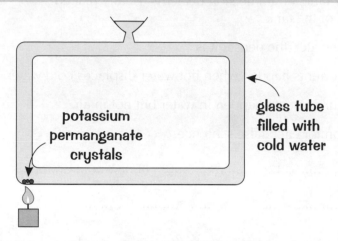

potassium
permanganate
crystals

glass tube
filled with
cold water

a)   Draw arrows on the diagram to show which way the water moves.

b)   Explain what happens to the water above the heat to cause the convection current.

....

....

....

....

....

Q5   Sam uses the apparatus shown to investigate heat transfer in water.

He heats the middle of the tube with a Bunsen flame.
The ice at the top of the tube melts quickly,
but the ice at the bottom does not melt.

**Ice floating
at the top**

**Glass tube full
of cold water**

**Ice weighted
so it stays at
the bottom**

What does this experiment show about conduction and
convection in water? Explain your answer.

....

....

....

<u>**Top Tips:**</u>   Remember, convection only happens in fluids (liquids and gases), conduction
happens fastest in solids, but <u>all</u> objects emit and absorb heat radiation.

Condensation and Evaporation

Q1 Complete the passage using the words given below. You will not have to use all the words.

kinetic energy   heats up   liquid   attractive   light energy   solid   repulsive   cools

Condensation is when a gas turns into a .... As a gas

....................................., the particles in the gas slow down and lose ....

The particles are pulled closer together by the .... forces between the

particles. If the particles get close enough together, then condensation takes place.

Q2 a) Tick the boxes to show whether the sentences are true or false.

True False

i) Evaporation is when particles escape from a liquid.

☐ ☐

ii) Particles can only evaporate from a liquid at temperatures above the liquid's boiling point.

☐ ☐

iii) Only the speed of a particle affects whether it can escape a liquid.

☐ ☐

b) Write a correction for each false sentence.

....

....

Q3 Explain why your body **sweats more** when you do exercise or get hot. You should talk about particles in your answer.

....

....

....

....

....

Q4 List **two** factors that would **increase** the **rate** of each of the following:

a) evaporation of a liquid.

....

....

b) condensation of a gas.

....

....

Rate of Heat Transfer

Q1   Radiators are used to transfer heat to their surroundings.

a)   Why do radiators have a large surface area?

....

b)   Explain why a radiator would transfer heat quicker to a **metal spoon**
      in contact with it, than to the **air** surrounding it.

....

....

Q2   List four features of a **vacuum flask** that reduce non-useful heat transfers.
            State whether each reduces conduction, convection or radiation.

1...

2...

3...

4...

Plastic cap filled with cork

Shiny mirrored surfaces

Vacuum

Sponge

Air

Plastic case

Q3   Mr Pink has a copper hot water tank with an electric **immersion heater** in it.
            The hot water tank **loses heat** from its **walls** by radiation, conduction and convection.
            Complete the table below, showing how to **reduce non-useful** heat transfers from the tank's walls.

Type of Transfer	Suggested improvements to reduce heat loss
Radiation	
Conduction	
Convection	

Which fluid will move and carry heat away?
Where will it go, and how could you stop it?

Physics 1a — Energy

Rate of Heat Transfer

Q4 Humans and animals have ways to help them control their heat transfer.

a) Explain why the hairs on your skin 'stand up' when you're cold.

....

....

b) Explain why some people's skin goes pink when they're hot.

....

....

Q5 The picture shows two different types of fox.

a) Identify which fox lives in a cold Arctic region and which lives in a desert.

i) Fox A ....

ii) Fox B ....

b) Explain how the difference in the size of the ears of the two foxes helps each of them to survive in its natural habitat.

....

....

....

Q6 Hayley measured some cubes to find out their surface area to volume ratio. Her results are shown in the table.

a) Calculate the **surface area : volume ratio** for each cube and write your answers in the table.

Just divide the surface area by the volume.

Length of cube side (cm)	Surface area of cube (cm^2)	Volume of cube (cm^3)	Surface area: volume ratio
2	24	8	
4	96	64	
6	216	216	
8	384	512	
10	600	1000	

b) As the cube size becomes larger, what happens to the value of the **surface area : volume ratio**?

....

c) Would you expect the smallest cube (length 2 cm) or the largest cube (length 10 cm) to change temperature more quickly? Explain your answer.

....

d) Use your answers above to explain why car engines often have 'fins'.

....

....

Physics 1a — Energy

Energy Efficiency in the Home

Q1   Heat is lost from a house through its **roof**, **walls**, **doors** and **windows**.

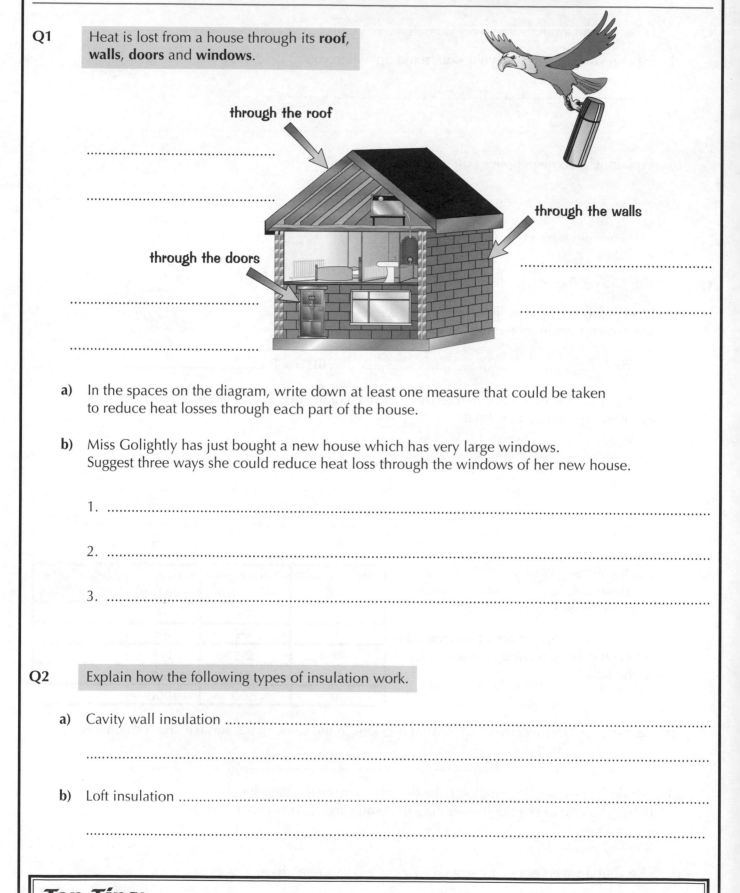

through the roof

through the walls

through the doors

a)   In the spaces on the diagram, write down at least one measure that could be taken to reduce heat losses through each part of the house.

b)   Miss Golightly has just bought a new house which has very large windows. Suggest three ways she could reduce heat loss through the windows of her new house.

1. ....

2. ....

3. ....

Q2   Explain how the following types of insulation work.

a)   Cavity wall insulation ....

....

b)   Loft insulation ....

....

Top Tips: If you want to build a new house, there are regulations about making it energy efficient — that's one reason why a lot of new houses have quite small windows. If you live in an old house, you can sometimes get a grant to cover the cost of installing extra insulation.

Energy Efficiency in the Home

Q3 Mr Tarantino wants to buy **double glazing** for his house, but the salesman tries to sell him insulated window shutters instead. He says it is cheaper and more **cost-effective**.

	Double glazing	Insulated window shutters
Initial Cost	£3000	£1200
Annual Saving	£60	£20
Payback time	50 years	

a) Calculate the **payback time** for insulated shutters and write it in the table.

b) Is the salesman's advice correct? Give reasons for your answer.

....

....

Q4 Gary is choosing between two brands of loft insulation material.
Brand A has a U-value of 0.15 W/m²K. Brand B has a U-value of 0.2 W/m²K.

a) What do U-values measure?

....

b) If both brands are the same price, which brand should Gary buy? Explain your answer.

....

....

Q5 Shona, Tim, Meena and Alison are discussing what 'cost-effectiveness' means.

Cost-effectiveness means having a short payback time. **Shona**

Cost-effectiveness means getting good value for your money. **Alison**

Cost-effectiveness means getting a job done for a low price. **Tim**

Cost-effectiveness just means not wasting energy. **Meena**

a) Whose explanations do you think are right? Circle their names.

Shona   Alison   Tim   Meena

b) Explain why the method with the shortest payback time is **not** always the best one to choose.

....

....

....

Specific Heat Capacity

Q1 a) What is **specific heat capacity**?

....

b) Agatha has 1 kg samples of two substances — A and B. Substance **A** has a **higher** specific heat capacity than substance B. Both samples cool down by 10 °C. Which will release more heat — A or B? Circle the correct answer.

Substance A

Substance B

Q2 To the right is a table with a list of **materials** and their **specific heat capacities**. Use the information in the table to help you answer the questions below.

Material	Specific heat capacity (J/kg°C)
Concrete	880
Oil	2000
Mercury	139
Water	4200
Copper	380

a) Which of the materials is used in storage heaters?

....

b) Which material is usually used to transfer heat around central heating systems? Explain why this material is the best one to use.

....

....

Q3 Mildred thinks she could make her hot water bottle more efficient by filling it with **mercury**, which has a specific heat capacity of **139 J/kg°C**. The specific heat capacity of water is **4200 J/kg°C**.

Work out the **difference** in energy released by two litres of mercury cooling from 70 °C to 20 °C and two litres of water cooling from 70 °C to 20 °C. (2 l of mercury has a mass of 27.2 kg. 2 l of water has a mass of 2 kg.)

Don't try this at home — mercury's toxic at any temperature.

....

....

....

....

Q4 A piece of copper is heated to **90 °C** and then lowered into a beaker of water which is at **20 °C**. The copper transfers **3040 J** of energy to the water before it is removed. The temperature of the copper after it is removed is **50 °C**. The specific heat capacity of copper is **380 J/kg°C**.

Calculate the **mass** of the copper. ....

....

....

Energy Transfer

Q1   Use the words below to fill in the gaps.

dissipated   transferred   created   conservation

The Principle for the .... of Energy says:

Energy can be .... usefully from one form to another, stored or

.... — but it can never be .... or destroyed.

Q2   Complete the following **energy transfer diagrams**. The first one has been done for you.

A solar water heating panel: ....light energy............   →   ....heat energy............

a)   A gas cooker: ....   →   heat and light energy

b)   An electric buzzer: electrical energy   →   ....

c)   A television screen: ....   →   ....

Q3   The diagram shows a **steam locomotive**.

a)   What form(s) of energy are there in the:

i)   coal ....

ii)   hot steam (which powers the engine) ....

b)   Describe two **energy transfers** which take place on the locomotive.

1...

2...

Q4   Bruce is practising weightlifting.

a)   When Bruce holds the bar still, above his head, what kind of energy does the weight have?

....

b)   Bruce had porridge for breakfast. Describe how the chemical energy in his porridge is transferred into the energy of the weight identified in part a).

....

....

c)   When Bruce lets go of the weight, what happens to its energy?

....

Energy Transfer

Q5 For each of the electrical appliances below, draw a line to the form of useful energy it is designed to produce.

Electric Fan

Iron

Bedside table lamp

electrical energy

heat energy

kinetic energy

sound energy

light energy

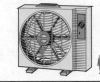

CGP's biggest fan

Q6 When an archer shoots an arrow into the air several **energy transfers** take place. The table below shows these transformations, but in the wrong order. Number the energy transformations from 1 to 5 to show the correct order.

Order	Energy transfers
	Energy stored in the pulled bow and string is transferred into kinetic energy.
	The arrow loses gravitational potential energy and gains kinetic energy as it falls to earth.
	Chemical energy in the archer's muscles is transferred into elastic potential energy.
1	Chemical energy from the archer's food is stored in his muscles.
	As it goes upwards the arrow loses kinetic energy and gains gravitational potential energy.

Q7 Each of the following sentences is incorrect. Write a correct version of each one.

a) In a battery-powered torch, the battery transfers **electrical energy** into **light energy**.

....

b) A **wind turbine** transfers **kinetic energy** into **electrical energy** only.

....

c) A wind-up toy car transfers **chemical energy** into **kinetic energy** and **sound energy**.

....

Q8 Write down the name of an appliance which transfers:

a) electrical energy into **sound energy** ....

b) light energy into **electrical energy** ....

c) electrical energy into **heat** and **kinetic energy** ....

Efficiency of Machines

Q1   Fill in the gaps using the correct words from the list below.

heat	light	input	create	output	total	useful	fraction	transfer

A **machine** is a device which can .... energy. Some of the energy

supplied to the machine is transferred into .... output energy.

But some energy is always wasted — often as .... or sound energy.

The **efficiency** of a **machine** is the .... of the **total energy**

.... that is transferred into useful energy ....

Q2   Here is an **energy flow diagram** for an electric lamp. Complete the following sentences.

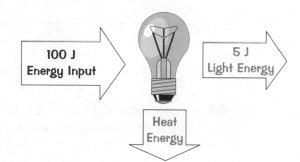

a)   The **total energy input** is .... J

b)   The **useful energy output** is .... J

c)   The amount of energy **wasted** is .... J

Q3   Complete the table below.

Appliance	Total Energy Input (J)	Useful Energy Output (J)	Efficiency
1	2000	1500	
2		2000	0.50
3	4000		0.25

Q4   A kettle has a power rating of 2000 W.
If it's 90% efficient, calculate its useful power output.

....

....

....

Efficiency of Machines

Q5   Tina was investigating a model **winch** —
a machine that uses an electric motor to lift objects.

Tina calculated that, in theory, **10 J** of electrical energy would be needed
to lift a **boot** 50 cm off a table. She then tried lifting the boot with the
winch, and found that, actually, **20 J** of electrical energy was used.

Why did the winch use so much more electrical energy in practice?
In your answer, include an explanation of what happened to the 'extra' 10 joules.

....

....

....

....

Q6   Sajid hopes his new MP3 player is better than his old one.
He decides to test which one is more **efficient**. He puts new
batteries in both MP3 players and switches them on. Then he
times how long they each play for before the batteries run out.

a)   How can he compare the **useful energy outputs**?

....

....

....

....

b)   Write down two things Sajid must do to make it a **fair test**.

....

....

c)   Player A lasts for 3 hours and Player B lasts for 4 hours.
Write a **conclusion** for Sajid's experiment.

....

....

....

Efficiency of Machines

Q7 Cars use **heat exchangers** to use some of the 'waste' heat energy produced by the car's engine.

Describe **one** way this heat energy can be used.

....

....

....

Q8 Clive is researching different kinds of electric light bulb. He finds the following information.

	Low-energy bulb	Ordinary bulb
Electrical energy input per second (J)	15	60
Light energy output per second (J)	1.4	1.4
Cost	£3.50	50p
Typical expected lifetime	8 years	1 year
Estimated annual running cost	£1.00	£4.00

Hint — most people don't like wasting money.

a) Write down two reasons for choosing a **low-energy** light bulb.

1) ....

2) ....

b) Write down two reasons why Clive might prefer to buy an ordinary bulb.

1) ....

2) ....

Top Tips: So... efficiency = good, waste = bad. Got it? Good. Remember — there's always a sneaky bit of waste energy produced by all machines, so nothing is 100% efficient. Some machines have heat exchangers to use wasted heat energy to do other things — clever, huh?

<u>Energy Transformation Diagrams</u>

Q1   This diagram shows the energy changes in a **toy crane**. The diagram is drawn to scale.

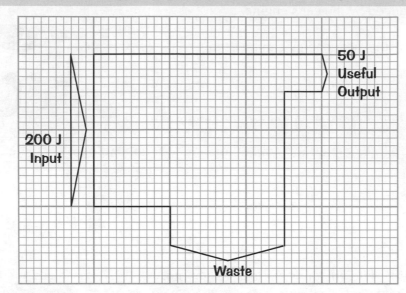

a)   How much energy is **one small square** worth? .... J

b)   How much energy is **wasted**? .... J

Q2   Professor Bean is testing a new **high-efficiency** car engine.
He finds that for every 100 J of energy supplied to the engine, 75 J is transformed into **kinetic energy** in the moving car, 5 J is wasted as **sound energy** and the rest is turned into **heat energy**.

On the graph paper below, draw an **energy transformation diagram** to illustrate his results.

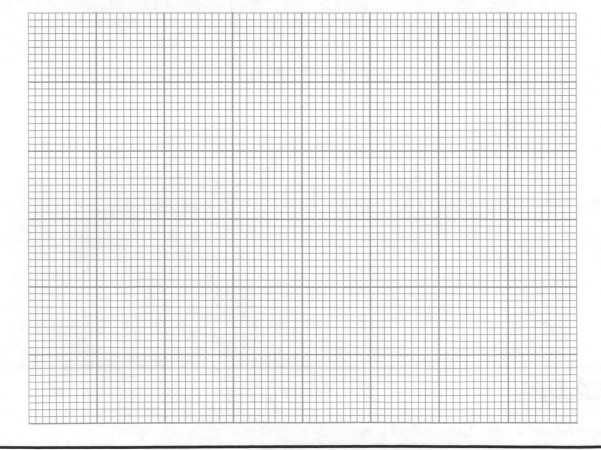

Physics 1a — Energy

Energy Transformation Diagrams

Q3 Liam measured the energy input and outputs for a model **electrical generator**.
He drew this diagram to show his results.

Describe two mistakes Liam has made on his diagram, and suggest how to correct them.

100 J kinetic energy

75 J electrical energy

100 J heat energy wasted

1...

....

....

2..

....

Q4 The Sankey diagram below is for a **winch** — a machine which **lifts** objects on hooks and cables.

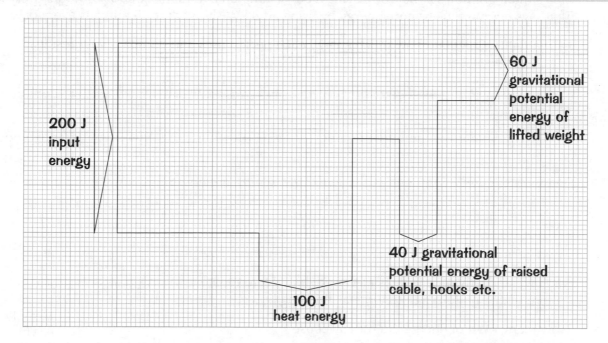

200 J input energy

60 J gravitational potential energy of lifted weight

40 J gravitational potential energy of raised cable, hooks etc.

100 J heat energy

a) What is the total amount of energy **wasted**? .... J

b) How much useful **gravitational energy** is produced? .... J

c) Calculate the **efficiency** of the winch. Give your answer as a decimal.

Efficiency = Useful Energy Output ÷ Total Energy Input

....

....

The Cost of Electricity

Q1   Boris puts his **2 kW** electric heater on for 3 hours.

a)   Calculate how many **kilowatt-hours** of electrical energy the heater uses.

Energy used = ...

b)   Boris gets his electricity supply from Ivasparkco. They charge 14p per kilowatt-hour.
Work out the **cost** of the energy calculated in part (a).

....

....

Q2   Tick the box next to the correct cost of using a **100 W** lamp for **10 hours**, if electrical energy costs **11.3p per kWh**.

You need to turn 100 W into kilowatts first.

☐ £1.13   ☐ 22.6p   ☐ 11.3p

Q3   Tina's mum grumbles at her for leaving a 60 W lamp on overnight — about 9 hours every night. Tina says her mum uses **more energy** by using an 8 kW shower for 15 minutes every day.

Is Tina right? Calculate how much energy each person uses and compare your results.

....

....

....

....

Q4   Mr Havel recently received his electricity bill. Unfortunately, he tore off the bottom part to write a shopping list.

a)   How many **kWh** of energy did Mr Havel use in the three months from June to September?

....

b)   What would the bill have said for 'total cost'?

....

....

Customer : Havel, V

Date	Meter Reading (kWh)
11 06 06	34259
10 09 06	34783

Total Cost @ 9.7p per kWh

The Cost of Electricity

Q5   **Pumped storage** power stations work by using **off-peak** electricity to pump water into a holding reservoir at night. In the daytime they release water from the reservoir to generate electricity, which is then sold to the National Grid at **peak rate** prices. The table below shows data for a typical pumped storage power station.

	Night time (input)	Daytime (output)
Running time	7 hours	5 hours
Power	275 MW	288 MW
Cost per kWh	3.7p	7.2p

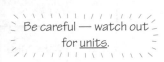

Be careful — watch out for <u>units</u>.

a)   Calculate the cost of electricity used in the night time operation.

....

....

b)   Calculate the value (in £) of the electricity generated in the daytime operation.

....

....

Q6   Mr Macintosh wants to work out how much **energy** he could save if he turned all his electrical appliances off overnight, instead of leaving them on standby.

On Tuesday night, he leaves all his appliances on **standby**. He takes a meter reading at **9pm** before going to bed and at **9am** the next morning when he wakes up. On Thursday night he **repeats** the experiment, but this time he **turns off** all his appliances.

Tuesday: Reading at 9pm	Wednesday: Reading at 9am		Thursday: Reading at 9pm	Friday: Reading at 9am
1 3 5 9 2 . 4 2 kWh	1 3 5 9 8 . 6 3 kWh		1 3 6 4 6 . 6 8 kWh	1 3 6 4 9 . 4 1 kWh
Appliances on standby			Appliances turned off	

Calculate the amount of energy Mr Macinstosh saved by turning off his electrical appliances overnight, rather than leaving them on standby.

....

....

....

Choosing Electrical Appliances

Q1   Two different types of power drill and some of their features are shown below.

Mains Powered Drill

Power output: 1.2 kW

Battery Powered Drill

Power output: 200 W

Battery Life: 8 hours

Suggest **two** reasons someone might choose to buy the battery
powered drill instead of the mains powered drill.

....

....

Q2   A **battery powered lamp** takes **6 hours** to charge fully when connected to
a **400 W** power supply. This gives the lamp enough energy for **8 hours** of use.
A **mains powered** lamp has a power rating of **1.6 kW**.

a)   If both lamps are used for 8 hours, calculate the difference in the amount of energy used.
Give your answer in kWh.

....

....

....

b)   If the cost of electricity is 12p per kWh, calculate the difference in cost of using both lamps for 8 hours.

....

c)   Suggest why somebody going on a camping trip might choose to buy a wind-up lamp instead of the
mains powered or battery powered lamps described above.

....

....

Q3   **Access to electricity** can improve people's **standard of living** in developing countries.

Give two examples of how electricity can help improve **public health** in developing countries.

1. ....

2. ....

Mixed Questions — Physics 1a

Q1   Paul is looking to buy some cavity wall insulation to reduce heat loss from his house.

a)   Explain how cavity wall insulation works.

....

....

b)   Should Paul look for cavity wall insulation with a high or a low U-value? Explain your answer.

....

....

c)   Paul has noticed he often gets condensation on the inside of his windows.
He is considering whether to get them double glazed.

Explain in terms of particles why the condensation happens.

....

....

....

Q2   Ben sets up an experiment as shown. He records the temperature
readings on thermometers A and B every two minutes.

The graph below shows Ben's results
for thermometer **B**.

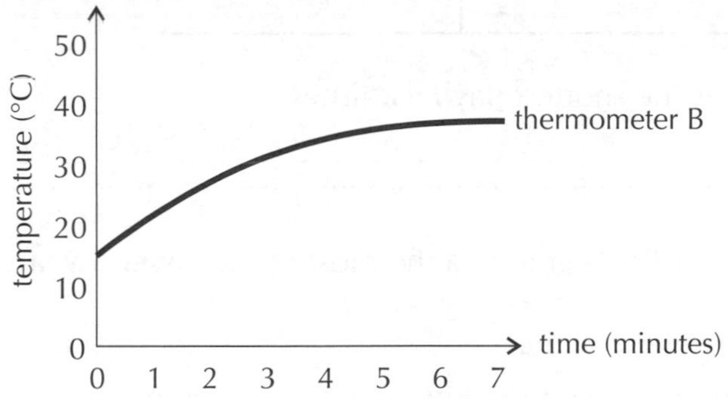

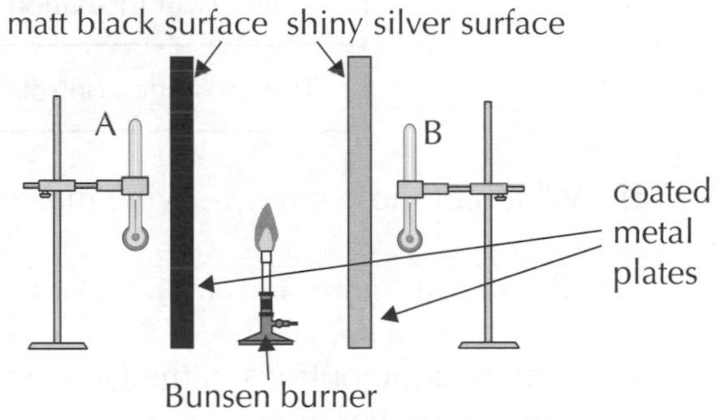

a)   On the diagram above, sketch the graph you would expect for thermometer **A**.

b)   Explain the differences between the two graphs.

....

....

....

c)   Complete the energy transfer diagram below for the Bunsen burner used in Ben's experiment.

....   →   ....

Mixed Questions — Physics 1a

Q3   Steve has bought a new fridge-freezer.

a)   Steve's new fridge-freezer has its freezer compartment above the refrigerator.
How does this arrangement encourage **convection currents** in the main body of the fridge?

....

....

b)   The fridge-freezer has a power of 500 W. Steve's electricity costs him 15p per kWh.
How much does it cost Steve to have the fridge-freezer switched on for a whole day (24 hours)?

....

....

....

Q4   Eric investigates ways of saving energy in his grandmother's house. He calculates the annual savings that could be made on his grandma's fuel bills, and the cost of doing the work.

Work needed	Annual Saving (£)	Cost of work (£)
Hot water tank jacket	15	15
Draught-proofing	65	70
Cavity wall insulation	70	560
Thermostatic controls	25	120

a)   Which of these energy-saving measures has the shortest **payback time**?

....

b)   Which of the options in the table would save Eric's grandma the most money **over 5 years**?
Show your working.

....

....

....

c)   Erik's grandma likes to have a hot bath in the evenings. How much energy is needed to heat 90 kg of water from 14 °C to 36 °C ? (The specific heat capacity of water is 4200 J/kg°C.)

....

....

....

Mixed Questions — Physics 1a

Q5 In one coal-fired power station, for every **1000 J** of energy input to the power station, 100 J is wasted in the **boiler**, 500 J is wasted in the **cooling water** and 50 J is wasted in the **generator**.

a) What **type** of energy is contained in the **coal**? ....

b) On the grid below, draw a detailed energy transformation diagram for this power station.

c) Calculate the **efficiency** of the power station.

....

....

Q6 Heat sinks are devices often used in computer circuits to transfer heat away from hot components.

a) Explain why heat sinks have **fins**.

....

....

b) Heat sinks are usually made of metal.

i) Why are metals **good conductors** of heat?

....

ii) Describe how heat is **transferred** from the hot end of a piece of metal to the cool end.

....

....

....

Energy Sources & Power Stations

Q1   In a coal-fired power station, there are several steps involved in making electricity. Number these steps in the right order.

☐ Hot steam rushes through a turbine and makes it spin.

☐ Electricity is produced by the spinning generator.

☐ Coal is burned to release heat.

☐ The spinning turbine makes the generator spin too.

☐ Water is heated in a boiler and turned to steam.

Q2   Nuclear power stations provide about 20% of the UK's electrical energy.

a)   How do uranium and plutonium provide heat energy?

....

b)   Uranium and plutonium are both non-renewable sources of energy. Explain what this means.

....

....

Q3   Use the words in the following list, to complete the paragraph below.

non-renewable   **kinetic**   **chemical**   **electrical**   **fossil**   **heat**

Most power stations use .... sources of energy, such as coal,

oil or gas. These .... fuels are initially burnt in a boiler.

This converts the .... energy in the fuel to .... energy.

A turbine then converts this energy into .... energy, which, in turn is

converted to .... energy by a generator.

This energy feeds into the national grid ready to be distributed to consumers.

Q4   Suggest a reason why wind and solar power are less reliable sources of energy than fossil fuels.

....

....

Top Tips: Make sure you know the difference between renewable and non-renewable energy sources, plus the different types of each. Then the exam will be a breeze — like wind through a turbine.

Renewable Energy Sources (1)

Q1   People often object to wind turbines being put up near to where they live.

   a)   List three reasons why they might object.

     1)..

     2)..

     3)..

   b)   List three arguments in favour of using wind turbines to generate electricity.

     1)..

     2)..

     3)..

Q2   Explain the advantages and disadvantages of using **solar cells** to generate electricity.

....

....

....

Q3   Renewable sources are often used for **small scale** production of electricity.

   a)   Explain why they're useful for this purpose.

....

....

   b)   A farmer on a remote farm uses a wind turbine to generate his electricity. He generates more electricity than he needs, and wants to connect his wind turbine to the national grid so he can sell his spare electricity. However, no electricity companies want to supply the connection and buy the excess energy. Suggest a reason for this.

....

....

Renewable Energy Sources (2)

Q1 Lynn and Hua are using the apparatus below to investigate how hydroelectric power works.

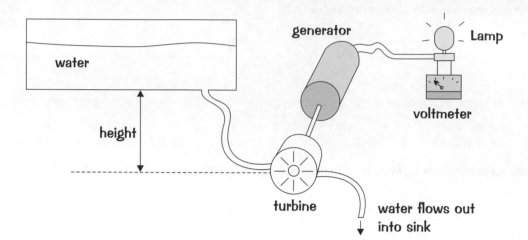

They put the tank at several different heights and recorded the voltage from the generator.

Height of tank (cm)	300	250	200	150	100
Voltage (V)	3.1	2.0	1.1	0.6	0.2
Brightness of lamp	bright	normal	dim	just lit	not lit

a) Why did they measure the **voltage** instead of just noting the brightness of the lamp?

....

b) They predicted that the energy generated would be **proportional** to the height of the tank. Do their results support this prediction? Explain your answer.

Their results **support / do not support** their prediction because ....

....

Q2 These sentences explain how pumped storage works. Put them in the right order by numbering them 1 to 4.

☐ Water at a high level stores energy until it is needed.

☐ At peak times, when demand is highest, water is allowed to flow downhill, powering turbines and generating electricity.

☐ At night big power stations make more electricity than is needed.

☐ Spare electricity is used to pump water from reservoirs at a low level to others at a high level.

Renewable Energy Sources (2)

Q3 Match up the beginnings and ends of the sentences. In one case, two matches are possible.

| Big coal-fired power stations deliver energy... | when it is needed. |

| Pumped storage power stations deliver energy... | all the time. |

| Hydroelectric power stations deliver electricity... | that they have previously stored. |

Q4 At a public meeting, people are sharing their views about hydroelectric power.

We should use hydroelectric power more — it doesn't cause any pollution.

And it gives us loads of free energy.

But it makes a terrible mess of the countryside.

At least it's reliable — it always gives us electricity when we need it.

Brian   **Hillary**   **Sue**   **Liz**

Say whether you agree or disagree with each person's view, and explain your reasons.

a) I agree / disagree with Brian because ....

....

b) I agree / disagree with Hillary because ....

....

c) I agree / disagree with Sue because ....

....

d) I agree / disagree with Liz because ....

....

e) Outline two **advantages** of hydroelectric power which were not mentioned at the public meeting.

1)...

2)...

f) Outline two **disadvantages** of hydroelectric power not mentioned at the meeting.

1)...

2)...

Renewable Energy Sources (3)

Q1   Tick the boxes to show whether each statement applies to
wave power or **tidal** power or **both**.

Wave Tidal

a)   Is usually used in estuaries.   ☐ ☐

b)   Suitable for small-scale use.   ☐ ☐

c)   Is a reliable way to generate electricity.   ☐ ☐

d)   The amount of energy generated depends on the weather.   ☐ ☐

e)   The amount of energy generated depends on the time of the month and year.   ☐ ☐

Q2   **Tidal barrages** can be used to generate electricity.   *What happens to make turbines go round?*

a)   Explain how a tidal barrage works.

....

....

....

b)   Give two reasons why people might object to a tidal barrage being built.

1..

2..

Q3   **Wave-powered generators** can be very useful around islands, like Britain.

a)   Number these sentences 1 to 6, to explain how a wave-powered generator works.

☐   The spinning generator makes electricity.

☐   The moving air makes the turbine spin.

☐   The water goes down again.

☐   Air is sucked downwards, spinning the turbine the other way and generating more power.

☐   A wave moves water upwards, forcing air out towards a turbine.

☐   The spinning turbine drives a generator.

b)   Give two possible problems with using wave power.

1..

2..

Renewable Energy Sources (4)

Q1 Use the words below to complete the following paragraph.

woodchips   fossil fuels   ethanol   water

steam   turbines   methane

Biofuels are used to generate electricity in a similar way to ....

Biofuels are burnt to heat .... and make .... which is used

to drive .... to power generators and make electricity.

Biofuels can be solids (e.g. ....), liquids (e.g. ....) or

gases (e.g. ....).

Q2 Describe how electricity is generated using geothermal energy.

....

....

....

Q3 Explain why biofuels are a 'renewable' source of energy.

....

....

Q4 Tick the boxes to show whether these statements about **geothermal** energy are true or false.

True False

a) Set-up costs are low.

b) It is possible in any country in the world.

c) There are lots of associated environmental problems.

d) Geothermal power stations use steam to drive turbines.

> **Top Tips:** Biofuels and geothermal energy are both renewable energy sources. One is steam coming from underground, and the other is burning stuff like wood and cow muck. How lovely.

Energy Sources and the Environment

Q1 Draw lines to match up each environmental problem below with something that causes it.

Acid rain

Climate change

Dangerous radioactive waste

Spoiling of natural landscapes

Releasing CO_2 by burning fossil fuels

Coal mining

Sulfur dioxide formed by burning oil and coal

Using nuclear power

Q2 Lisa says: "Using nuclear power to make electricity is too dangerous."
Ben says: "Using fossil fuels is even more dangerous in the long run."

Who do you think is right? Explain your answer.

....

....

....

Q3 Biofuels are often described as being 'carbon neutral'.

Explain why burning biofuels is 'carbon neutral'.

....

....

....

Q4 'Carbon capture' reduces the impact of burning fossil fuels on the environment.

a) Describe what is meant by the term 'carbon capture'?

....

....

b) Give an example of how the captured carbon dioxide can be stored.

....

Comparison of Energy Resources

Q1 Which of the following fossil fuel power stations has the shortest start-up time? Circle your answer.

Coal   Oil   Gas

Q2 The city of Fakeville decides to replace its old coal-fired power station. They have to choose between using gas, nuclear, wind or geothermal.

Give one **disadvantage** of each choice:

a) **Gas** ....

....

b) **Nuclear** ....

....

c) **Wind** ....

....

d) **Geothermal** ....

....

Q3 This is part of a leaflet produced by the pressure group 'Nuclear Is Not the Answer' (NINA).

Read the extract and answer the questions on the next page.

Imagine life without electricity. No lights, no computers, no TV... no kettles, no tea? Unthinkable. But that's what could happen when the oil and gas run out — because in the UK we generate about 75% of our electricity from power stations running on fossil fuels.

The Government has decided to build more nuclear power stations.
At NINA, we believe that nuclear is not the answer.

Nuclear power stations generate power, yes, but they also generate huge piles of highly radioactive waste. No one has any idea how to get rid of this waste safely. So should we really be making more of it? Radioactive waste stays dangerous for hundreds of thousands of years. Would you be happy living near a nuclear fuel dump? That's not all — nuclear power stations, and the lethal waste they create, are obvious targets for terrorists. And, last but not least, building more nuclear power stations would cost the taxpayer billions.

The good news is, we don't need nuclear power. There are safer, cleaner ways to produce electricity — using renewable energy. Many people argue that renewables are unreliable — the wind doesn't always blow, for instance. Well, true, but tidal power is reliable — and we have hundreds of miles of coastline with tides washing in and out twice every day.

If you don't want your children to grow up in a nuclear-powered world, join NINA today.

<u>Comparison of Energy Resources</u>

a) Explain clearly why the author thinks that we could find ourselves without electricity.

....

....

b) Give two reasons why the author thinks nuclear power is **dangerous**.

1..

2..

c) Nuclear power stations are the most expensive type of power plant to **decommission**.

Explain what is meant by the term decommission.

....

....

d) The author suggests that tidal power is a **plentiful** and **reliable** source of energy. Do you agree? Explain your answer.

I **agree** / **disagree** because ....

....

....

e) Give two possible arguments **in favour** of nuclear power.

1..

....

2..

....

Electricity and the National Grid

Q1 Number these statements 1 to 5 to show the order of the steps that are needed to deliver energy to Mrs Miggins' house so that she can boil the kettle.

	An electrical current flows through power cables across the country.
	Mrs Miggins boils the kettle for tea.
	Electrical energy is generated in power stations.
	The voltage of the supply is raised.
	The voltage of the supply is reduced.

Q2 Electricity can be transmitted by either **overhead** or **underground cables**. Tick the appropriate box to answer each of the following questions:

	Overhead cables	Underground cables
a) Which **cost** more to set up?	☐	☐
b) Which require the most **maintenance**?	☐	☐
c) Which are the easiest to **repair**?	☐	☐
d) Which are most affected by **weather**?	☐	☐
e) Which are most **reliable**?	☐	☐
f) Which are the **easiest** to install?	☐	☐
g) Which cause the most disturbance to **land**?	☐	☐

Q3 Using **high voltages** in power cables means you need some **expensive** equipment.

a) Make a list of the main equipment you need for **high voltage transmission**.

....

....

b) Explain why it is still **cheaper** to use **high voltages** for transmission.

....

....

Top Tips: Wowsers. Overhead and underground cables are pretty darn interesting. Or maybe not. Either way, you need to know the pros and cons of both types of cable, soz.

Electricity and the National Grid

Q4 Each of the following sentences is incorrect.
Write a correct version of each.

a) The National Grid transmits energy at **high voltage** and **high current**.

....

b) A step-up transformer is used to **reduce the voltage** of the supply before electricity is transmitted.

....

c) Using a **high current** makes sure there is not much energy **wasted**.

....

....

Q5 The **National Grid** distributes electricity from power stations to the consumers.

a) Explain what is meant by the 'supply and demand' of electricity.

....

....

b) Describe **one** problem the National Grid faces concerning supply and demand.

....

c) Suggest **two** ways the National Grid can increase the supply of electricity.

....

....

d) Suggest **two** ways in which consumers can help reduce demand for electricity.

....

....

Top Tips: The key thing to remember is that high voltage means low current, which means the cables don't get so hot — so less energy is wasted. And while you're at it, the ways of matching supply with demand are really important to learn too. You might get asked about all this stuff in the exam, which is why we put it in our book. It wasn't just for fun. If you did have fun — good for you.

Physics 1b — Electricity and Waves

Wave Basics

Q1 Complete the sentence below by circling the correct word in each pair.

Waves transfer **energy / matter** without transferring any **energy / matter.**

Q2 There are **two ways** in which you can make waves on a **slinky** spring.

a) Which diagram shows a **transverse** wave, and which one shows a **longitudinal** wave?

Transverse: ....

Longitudinal: ....

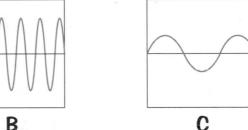

① ②

b) Write down one difference between these two types of wave.

....

....

Q3 Diagrams **A**, **B** and **C** represent electromagnetic waves.

A   **B**   **C**

a) Which two diagrams show waves with the same **frequency**? .... and ....

b) Which two diagrams show waves with the same **amplitude**? .... and ....

c) Which two diagrams show waves with the same **wavelength**? .... and ....

Q4 Which of the phrases below relate to **transverse** waves and which to **longitudinal**? Write '**T**' for transverse, and '**L**' for longitudinal.

☐ vibrations are at 90° to the direction of energy transfer   ☐ electromagnetic radiation

☐ sound waves   ☐ vibrations are along the same direction as the energy transfer

☐ produced by a slinky spring whose end is wiggled at 90° to the spring itself   ☐ ripples on water   ☐ produced by a slinky spring whose end is pushed and pulled towards and away from the rest of the spring

Wave Basics

Q5   All waves have a **frequency** and a **wavelength**.

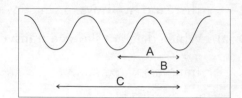

a)   What units are used to measure wavelength? ....

b)   What does it mean to say that "the frequency of a wave is 25 hertz"?

....

c)   The diagram shows a waveform.
         Which of A, B or C is the length of one whole wave?

....

Q6   There are six equations below, some of which are **incorrect**.
         Draw a big thick line through the ones that are incorrect.

Frequency = Speed × Wavelength

$$\text{Frequency} = \frac{\text{Wavelength}}{\text{Speed}}$$

$$\text{Wavelength} = \frac{\text{Speed}}{\text{Frequency}}$$

$$\text{Speed} = \frac{\text{Frequency}}{\text{Wavelength}}$$

Speed = Frequency × Wavelength

$$\text{Frequency} = \frac{\text{Speed}}{\text{Wavelength}}$$

Q7   **Green light** travels at 3×10^8 m/s and has a wavelength of about 5×10^{-7} m.

Calculate the **frequency** of green light. Give the correct unit in your answer.

....

....

Q8   Jason draws the graph on the right to show a wave
         with an **amplitude** of **4 m** and a **wavelength** of **2 m**.

a)   What has Jason done wrong?

....

....

b)   On the same set of axes, draw a wave with a **wavelength**
         of **5 m** and an **amplitude** of **3 m**.

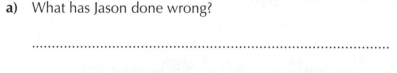

Q9   An ultraviolet wave has a frequency of 4.6×10^{15} Hz. It travels at a speed of 3×10^8 m/s.

Calculate the **wavelength** of the wave.

....

....

Wave Properties

Q1   Harriet spends at least an hour looking at herself in a **mirror** every day.
The image she sees is formed from light reflected by the mirror.

a)   What is meant by a "normal" when talking about reflection?

....

....

b)   Complete the diagram to show an
incident ray of light being reflected
by the mirror. Label the **angle of
incidence**, **i**, the **normal**, and
the **angle of reflection**, **r**.

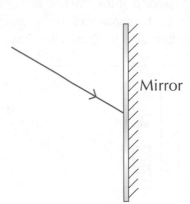

Mirror

Q2   The diagram below shows a pencil being reflected in a **plane mirror**.
Some of the rays have already been drawn in.

a)   On the diagram, draw in the rays
showing how light is reflected to form
an image of the **top** of the pencil.

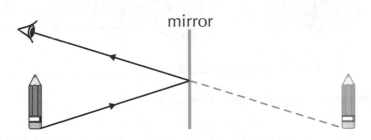

mirror

b)   Is the image in a plane mirror real or virtual? ....

c)   Is the image inverted or upright? ....

d)   The image of the pencil is **laterally inverted**. Explain what this means.

....

....

Top Tips: If you get asked a question about constructing ray diagrams, remember the
important rule for drawing reflections in a plane mirror: **angle of incidence = angle of reflection**.
Always use a **ruler** to draw your ray diagrams too — examiners love a line drawn with a ruler.

Refraction and Diffraction

Q1 Waves can be **diffracted**.

a) Explain what 'diffraction' means.

....

....

b) A ripple tank is used to study the behaviour of waves as they pass through gaps. The gap in diagram 1 is about the **same size** as the wavelength. The gap in diagram 2 is **much bigger**. Complete both diagrams to show what happens to the waves after they pass through the gaps.

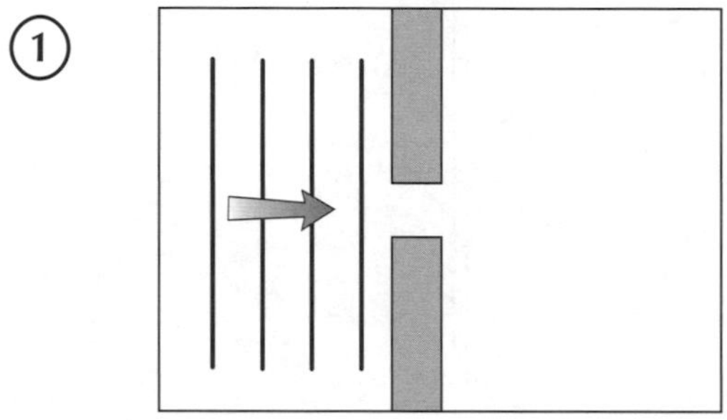

①

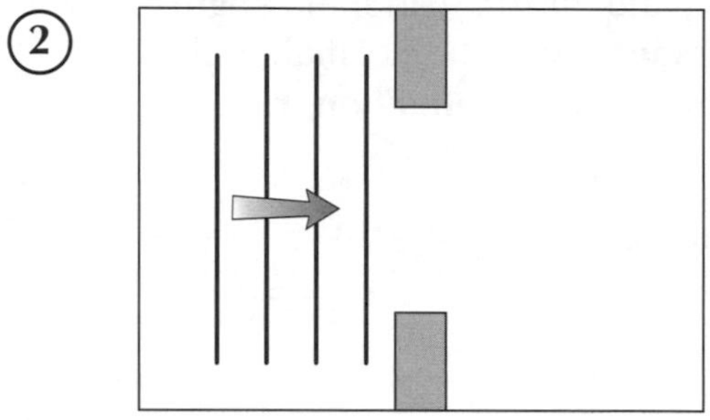

②

Q2 Diagrams A and B show plane **water waves** travelling from **deep** to **shallow** water in a ripple tank.

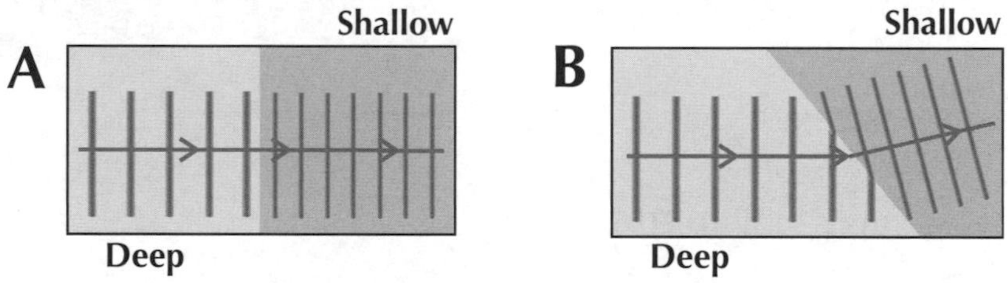

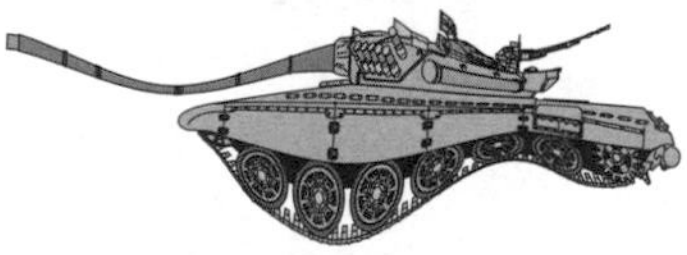

a) Which diagram shows the waves being **refracted**? ....

b) Why does refraction **not happen** in the other diagram?

....

c) Write a definition of **refraction**.

....

....

Q3 Why do you not see **light** diffract as it passes through a **doorway**?

....

....

EM Waves and Communication

Q1   The different types of **EM waves** form a spectrum.

a)   Use the words below to complete the table to show the seven types of EM waves:

Infrared   Gamma rays   Ultraviolet

X-rays   Radio waves   Microwaves

			VISIBLE LIGHT			
$1 \text{ m}-10^4 \text{ m}$	10^{-2} m (1 cm)	$10^{-5} \text{ m (0.01 mm)}$	10^{-7} m	10^{-8} m	10^{-10} m	10^{-15} m

b)   In which direction does the **energy** of the electromagnetic radiation **increase** across the table? Tick the box next to the correct answer.

☐   The energy of the waves **increases** from **left to right** across the table.

☐   The energy of the waves **increases** from **right to left** across the table.

Q2 a)   Tick the correct boxes to show whether each of the following statements is true or false.

True False

i)   Visible light travels faster in a vacuum than both X-rays and radio waves.   ☐ ☐

ii) All EM waves transfer matter from place to place.   ☐ ☐

iii) Radio waves have the shortest wavelength of all EM waves.   ☐ ☐

iv) All EM waves can travel through space.   ☐ ☐

b)   Write a correction for each false sentence.

....

....

....

....

Q3   Circle the letter next to the statements below that are true.

A   Long waves such as radio waves are good for transmitting information long distances.

B   Some wavelengths of radio wave are reflected by the ionosphere and come back to Earth.

C   Short-wave radio waves can be diffracted around hills.

D   To receive TV signals, you must be in the direct line of sight of the transmitter.

EM Waves and Communication

Q4   Complete the sentences below by circling the correct word in each pair.

EM waves with higher frequencies have **shorter / longer** wavelengths.

The **higher / lower** the frequency of an EM wave, the greater the energy of the wave.

Q5   The house shown below receives radio signals from a nearby transmitter, even though there is a mountain between the house and the transmitter.

radio transmitter

Use the words below to fill in the blanks in the passage.

ionosphere   short-wave   long-wave   FM

The house can receive .... signals because they can diffract around

the mountain. It also receives .... signals because they are

reflected by the .... However .... signals are not

received at the house as the transmitter is not in direct line of sight of the house.

Q6   Red and violet are at opposite ends of the spectrum of **visible** light.
Describe two things they have in common and two ways in which they differ.

....

....

....

....

EM Waves and Their Uses

Q1   Television remote controls use EM waves to communicate with the TV.

Underline the type of radiation used in wireless remote controls.

Gamma   **UV**   **Infrared**   **X-ray**

Q2   Gabrielle in Britain and Carwyn in Canada are talking by mobile phone.

Communications Satellite

NOT TO SCALE

Carwyn's phone

Gabrielle's phone

Atlantic Ocean

a)   Suggest why the satellite needs to be high above the Earth.

....

....

b)   Why are radio waves not used to communicate with satellites?

....

c)   What type of electromagnetic waves are used to communicate with satellites?

....

Q3   A **cable TV** company uses a large dish to collect TV signals from a satellite in space. It then sends these signals to houses along **optical fibres**.

a)   What type(s) of EM waves could be used to send the signals along the optical fibres?

....

b)   Describe how the EM radiation is transmitted down the optical fibre.

....

EM Waves and Their Uses

Q4   Explain how a microwave camera on a remote-sensing satellite can 'see' through clouds.

....

....

....

Q5   It has been suggested that using **mobile phones** could cause **brain tumours**. However, at the moment there is **no reliable evidence** to prove that this is or isn't the case.

a)   What type of radiation is used by mobile phones?

....

b)   What could happen to the **brain cells** of people who use mobile phones?

....

....

c)   Why do people still **take the risk** by using mobile phones?

....

....

....

Q6   Visible light is used for photography.

Briefly describe how a camera uses visible light to take a photo.

....

....

....

Top Tips: There are four main types of electromagnetic radiation used in communications technology — microwaves, radio waves, visible light and infrared radiation. Make sure you know the uses of each. Then as a reward, practice using infrared radiation by channel hopping with your remote.

Sound Waves

Q1   Sound waves are caused by **vibrations**.

Put the following sentences in the correct order to describe how the sound of a drumbeat is made and reaches our ears.

A   The vibration of the drum sets the air molecules next to it vibrating too.

B   We hear the sound when the vibrations in the air reach our ears.

C   When someone beats a drum, the skin on top of the drum vibrates.

D   A series of compressions and decompressions travel outwards through the air (or other medium) as a longitudinal wave.

Correct order: .... , ... , ... , ...

Q2   Choose from the words below to fill in the spaces in the passage.

high   low   vibrate

A sound wave makes air molecules .... If there are

many vibrations per second the frequency or pitch of the sound is

.... If there are only a few vibrations per second the pitch

of the sound is ....

Q3   Complete the sentences below by circling the correct word in each pair.

The bigger the **amplitude / frequency** of a sound wave, the **louder / quieter** the sound.

Q4   A bell is vibrating with a frequency of 2 kHz. How many times a second is it vibrating?

....

Q5   Most humans can hear sounds in the frequency range 20 Hz to 20 000 Hz.

a)   What is the frequency of a sound wave that has 30 compressions in one second?

....

b)   Put the following frequencies in order, from the lowest frequency to the highest.

3 MHz, 8 kHz, 630 Hz, 400 kHz, 5 Hz, 21 kHz

....

Sound Waves

Q6   Mina sings in her school choir. She practises both in her bedroom and in an empty practice room at school. She hears a difference in the sound of her voice, caused by a difference in echo.

a)   What is an echo?

....

....

b)   Why were there lots of echoes in the unfurnished practice room but not in her bedroom at home?

....

....

c)   Why is there a delay before you hear an echo?

....

....

Q7   In an experiment, a ringing alarm clock is placed in a glass bell jar. Air is sucked out of the jar by a vacuum pump.

a)   What happens to the sound and why?

....

....

b)   Why does the experiment work better if the alarm clock is placed on top of a block of foam?

....

....

Top Tips: I know what you're thinking — it's an outrage what these alarm clocks have to go through in the name of science. Why not calm yourself though, by making sure you know all the stuff about sound off the last two pages, like what an echo is and how pitch is determined by frequency.

The Origin of the Universe

Q1   Francesca is standing by a busy street when an ambulance rushes past, with its sirens blaring.

a)   As the ambulance moves away, how will the siren sound different to Francesca?
Underline the correct answer.

It will sound higher pitched   **It will sound lower pitched**

b)   What is the name of this effect?

....

c)   As the ambulance moves away, what happens to the
wavelength of the sound waves heard by Francesca?

....

d)   How would the frequency of the sound wave Francesca heard
have changed as the ambulance approached her?

....

Q2   Brian set up a microphone at his local railway station to record his favourite **train noises**.
He attached the microphone to an oscilloscope.

An express train passed through the station at a constant speed. Diagram A below shows the trace
on the monitor at 11:31:07, as the train **approached** Brian's microphone.

On diagram B, sketch
the trace Brian might have
seen as the train **left** the
station.

A

11:31:07

B

11:31:08

Q3   What **evidence** is there to support the idea that the universe is **expanding**?
Include a brief explanation of **red-shift** in your answer.

....

....

....

....

The Origin of the Universe

Q4   Many cosmologists believe that the universe began with a Big Bang.

a)   Briefly describe the Big Bang theory.

....

....

....

....

b)   According to the Big Bang theory, what is happening to space itself?

....

Q5   The Big Bang theory is currently the only theory that can explain
the existence of cosmic microwave background radiation (CMBR).

a)   What is cosmic microwave background radiation?

....

....

b)   How does the Big Bang theory explain CMBR?

....

....

....

....

Q6   The Big Bang theory can't explain everything about the universe.
Describe **one** limitation of the Big Bang theory.

....

....

....

Top Tips: Crikey, the question of how the universe started is a pretty big question. Make sure
you know all about the Big Bang theory and the evidence that supports it. It's interesting stuff, I reckon.

Mixed Questions — Physics 1b

Q1 The waves A, B and C represent **infrared**, **visible light** and **ultraviolet** radiation (not in that order).

a) Tick the box next to any of the following statements which are true.

☐ B represents ultraviolet radiation.

☐ The infrared wave has the largest amplitude.

☐ C has the highest frequency.

☐ A has the shortest wavelength.

b) Which of the following things do the three waves have in common? Circle the letter(s) of the correct answer(s).

A — They have the same frequency.

B — They are all transverse waves.

C — They transfer the same amount of energy.

D — They travel at the same speed in space.

Q2 A group of farmers live on a remote island, growing potatoes and farming llamas. They decide to put **solar cells** on the roofs of their houses and put up **wind turbines** in their fields.

a) Suggest why the farmers have chosen to use:

i) solar power ....

....

....

ii) wind power ....

....

....

b) What other renewable sources of energy could the farmers use?

....

Mixed Questions — Physics 1b

Q3   Radio Roary transmits **radio** signals with a wavelength of **1.5 km**.

a)   Calculate the **frequency** of Radio Roary's transmission. (Use speed = 3×10^8 m/s.)

....

....

b)   Mr Potts is on holiday in the Scottish Highlands. He follows England's progress in the cricket test match on Radio Roary, but he can't watch the coverage on television, because TV reception at the cottage is so poor.

Explain why Mr Potts gets **good** long-wave radio reception, but such **poor** TV reception.

....

....

Q4   A council are discussing plans to build a new power station.

a)   Give one advantage of nuclear power.

....

b)   Some council members are concerned about the effect fossil-fuel power stations have on the environment. How does carbon capture and storage technology help reduce these effects?

....

....

Q5   Infrared radiation is used by TV **remote controls**. Jake shows Peter that he can change the TV channel by pointing the remote control at a mirror on the opposite wall.

a)   What property of EM rays has Jake demonstrated? Circle the correct answer.

reflection   **refraction**   **diffraction**

b)   Draw a ray diagram below to show the path of the radiation emitted from the remote control to the TV.

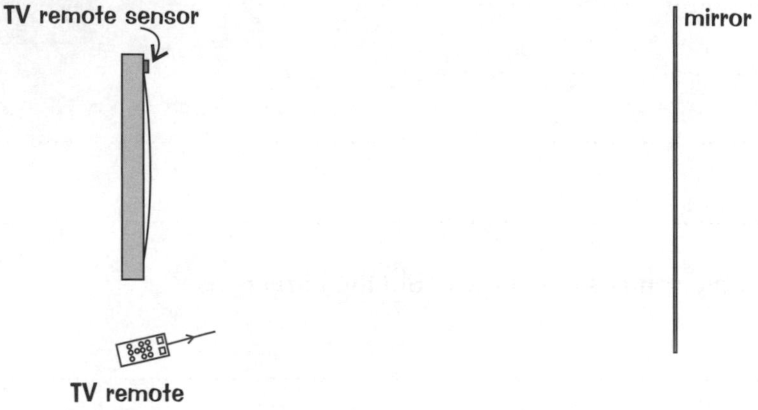

TV remote sensor

mirror

TV remote

Mixed Questions — Physics 1b

Q6 A coal-fired power station generates electricity throughout the day and night, even though there is less demand for electricity overnight.

a) Describe one way 'spare' night-time electricity can be used to store energy for later use.

....

....

....

b) List three things that could help the National Grid match supply with demand.

1. ....

2. ....

3. ....

Q7 Mobile phones use microwaves. These waves can spread out as they pass through a gap, or move past an object.

a) What is the **technical name** for this spreading out?

....

b) How does the **size** of the gap affect the **amount** that it spreads out?

....

c) Describe the **possible health risks** associated with using mobile phones.

....

....

Q8 A pebble is dropped into still water. Waves move out across the surface of the water. The wavelength is **2 cm** and the waves are generated at a rate of **10 per second**.

a) What is the **wavelength** in metres?

....

b) What is the **frequency** of the wave in Hz?

....

c) What is the **speed** of the wave?

....

<u>Mixed Questions — Physics 1b</u>

Q9   Electricity is generated in **power stations** and reaches our homes by a network of **power cables**.

a)   Describe how electricity is produced in a gas-fired power station.

....

....

....

....

b)   Natural gas is a fossil fuel. Burning it releases carbon dioxide and contributes to climate change.

i)   Suggest two alternative types of fuel which could be used to produce heat in power stations without contributing to climate change.

.... and ....

ii)   It is now possible to install solar cells and wind turbines on the roof of a house. Explain why few households in the UK could rely on these technologies for their electricity supply.

....

....

c) **i)**   Explain why electricity transmission cables are at very high voltages.

....

....

ii)   Explain why the high voltage of the cables is not dangerous for people using the electricity.

....

....

Q10   The diagram represents a **light wave** emitted from Cygnus A — a galaxy about 700 million light years from Earth.

a)   On the diagram, redraw the wave to show how it might appear to us on Earth because the light is **red-shifted**.

b)   Explain how red-shifts from distant and nearer galaxies provide evidence for the Big Bang theory.

....

....

....

Velocity and Distance-Time Graphs

Q1   The **monorail** at Buffers' Theme Park takes people from the visitor centre to the main park and back again. It travels at the same **speed** on the outward and return journeys.

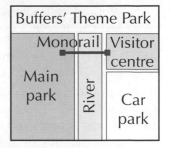

The monorail's velocity on the outward journey is 12 m/s. What is its velocity on the return journey?

....

Q2   Steve walked to football training only to find that he'd left his boots at home. He turned round and walked back home, where he spent 30 seconds looking for them. To make it to training on time he had to run back at twice his walking speed.

Below is an incomplete **distance-time graph** for Steve's journey.

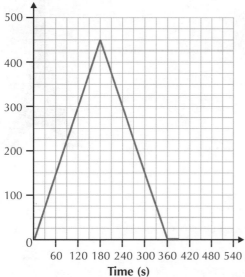

a)   How long did it take Steve to walk to training?

....

b)   Calculate Steve's speed (in m/s) as he walked to training.

....

....

c)   Complete the graph to show Steve's run back from his house to training (with his boots).

Q3   The speed limit for cars on motorways is 70 mph (about 31 m/s). A motorist was stopped by the police for speeding as she joined the motorway from a service station.

The distance-time graph on the right shows the car's acceleration. The motorist denied speeding. Was she telling the truth?

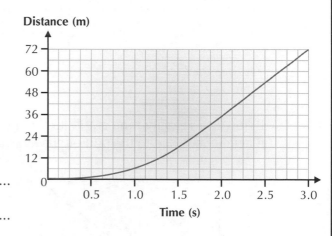

....

....

....

....

Top Tips: Velocity and speed are pretty much interchangeable in everyday language, but whereas speed is a scalar quantity with only magnitude, velocity is a vector quantity, with magnitude and direction.

54

Acceleration and Velocity-Time Graphs

Q1 The Go Go car company make gas-powered model cars.
One car accelerates from rest to 20 m/s in 3.5 s.

a) What is its acceleration?

....

b) The car is modified and now accelerates from 3 m/s to 20 m/s in 2.8 s.
Show that this modification has improved the car's acceleration.

....

....

Q2 An egg is dropped from the top of the Eiffel tower.
It hits the ground after 8 seconds, at a speed of 80 m/s.

a) Find the egg's acceleration. ....

b) How long did it take for the egg to reach 40 m/s?

....

Q3 A car accelerates at 2 m/s^2. After 4 seconds it reaches a speed of 24 m/s.

How fast was it going before it started to accelerate?

....

....

Q4 Below is a velocity-time graph for the descent of a lunar lander.
It accelerates due to the pull of gravity from the Moon.

Use the graph to calculate this acceleration.

....

....

....

Physics 2a — Motion, Energy and Electricity

Acceleration and Velocity-Time Graphs

Q5 Describe the **type of motion** happening at each of the labelled points on the velocity-time graph.

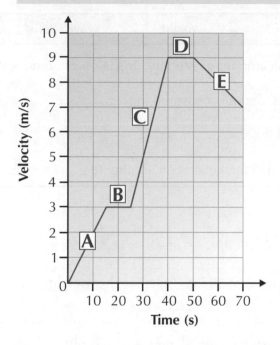

A ....

B ....

C ....

D ....

E ....

Q6 A bus driver saw a piglet asleep on the road **25 m** in front of him. It took him **0.75 seconds** to react and slam on the brakes. The **velocity-time graph** below shows the bus's deceleration.

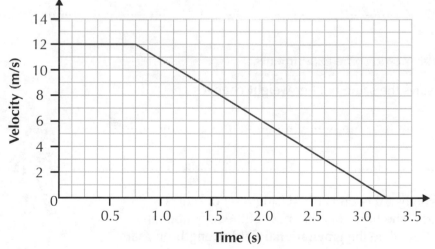

It helps to split the graph up into two smaller shapes.

Use the graph to work out whether the bus driver stopped before hitting the piglet.

....

....

Top Tips: Velocity-time graphs can be confusing — so don't rush them. Take your time to break the graph down into the different sections and figure out exactly what's happening at each stage.

Physics 2a — Motion, Energy and Electricity

Weight, Mass and Gravity

Q1   Fill in the gaps in the following paragraph using the words below:

kilograms	newtons	mass	weight	gravitational

The .... of an object is just the amount of 'stuff' it's made up of. It doesn't

change, regardless of where in the universe it is, and it's measured in ....

.... is a force and is measured in .... — it's the

.... force that one object (e.g. a planet) exerts on another (e.g. an apple).

Q2   Joni has been feeding her dog Fluffy a bit too much bacon. The vet decides he needs to go on a diet.

g = 10 N/kg

a)   Joni puts Fluffy on some scales and finds he has a mass of **58 kg**. Calculate his **weight**.

....

b)   After three weeks of Fluffy eating only 'Skinny Dog' biscuits, Joni weighs Fluffy by putting him in a sling and hanging him from a **newton meter**. He now has a weight of **460 N**. How much **mass** has he lost?

....

....

Q3   An astronaut goes to Mars to do some experiments.

a)   Explain why her **mass** stays the same but her **weight** changes.

....

....

Woohoo! Who needs diets? Just go to Mars...

b)   She takes a rock that weighs **50 N** on Earth. Using a set of scales designed for use on Earth, she finds that the mass of the rock appears to be **1.9 kg** on Mars. Calculate the **gravitational field strength** on Mars.

....

....

Top Tips: Gravity may be keeping you down to the earth, but compared to the other fundamental forces, it is actually **surprisingly weak**. Think about it — you have whole Earth pulling you downwards but you can jump and hop and skip away from it without too much effort. Then think about how much effort it can take to pull opposite ends of a small magnet apart. The fact is, **anything that has mass has gravity**, but objects have to be pretty humongous before anyone notices.

Resultant Forces

Q1 A teapot sits on a table.

a) Explain why it doesn't sink into the table.

....

b) Chris carelessly knocks the teapot off the table and it accelerates towards the floor.

   i) Explain whether the vertical forces are balanced.

   ....

   ii) The teapot hits the floor without breaking and bounces upwards.
   Name the force that causes the teapot to bounce upwards.

   ....

Q2 A bear rides a bike north at a constant speed.

a) Label the forces acting on the bear.

....

b) The bear brakes and slows down.
Are the forces balanced **as** he
slows down? If not, which
direction is the resultant force in?

....

....

....

Q3 The **force diagram** on the right shows a **train** pulling out of a station.

Calculate the resultant force acting on
the train in the following directions:

1 500 000 N

6 000 000 N

1 500 000 N

a) Vertical: ....

b) Horizontal: ....

1 500 000 N

Q4 State whether there is a resultant force in each of the following situations. Explain your answers.

a) A cricket ball slowing down as it rolls along the outfield.

....

b) A car going round a roundabout at a steady 30 mph.

....

c) A vase sat on a window ledge.

....

Forces and Acceleration

Q1 Use the words supplied to fill in the blanks in the paragraph below.

interact	resultant force	stationary	accelerates
opposite	constant	non-zero	balanced

If the forces on an object are ………….....………… , it's either …………..…………..

or moving at ………….....……….. speed. If an object has a …………..…………..

resultant force acting on it, it …………..………….. in the direction of the

…………..………….. . When two objects …………..………….. ,

the forces they exert on each other are equal and …………..…………. .

Q2 You're travelling home from school on a bus doing a steady speed in a straight line.
Which of the following is true? Tick the appropriate box.

☐   The driving force of the engine is bigger than friction and air resistance combined.

☐   There are no forces acting on the bus.

☐   The driving force of the engine is equal to friction and air resistance combined.

☐   A resultant force is required to keep the bus moving.

Q3 The diagram below shows the **forces** acting on an aeroplane.

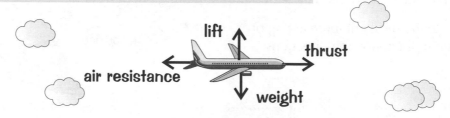

a) The aircraft is flying horizontally at a constant speed of 200 m/s. Which of the following
statements about the aeroplane is true? Circle the appropriate letter.

A   The thrust is bigger than the air resistance and the lift is bigger than the weight.

B   The thrust is smaller than the air resistance and the lift is equal to the weight.

C   The thrust is equal to the air resistance and the lift is equal to the weight.

D   The thrust is equal to the air resistance and the lift is bigger than the weight.

b) What happens to the forces as the plane descends for landing and slows down to 100 m/s?
Choose the correct options to complete the following statements:

i) The thrust is **greater than / less than / equal to** the air resistance.

ii) The lift is **greater than / less than / equal to** the weight.

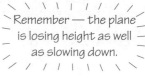
Remember — the plane
is losing height as well
as slowing down.

Forces and Acceleration

Q4 Put these cars in order of increasing driving force.

Car	Mass (kg)	Maximum acceleration (m/s^2)
Disraeli 9000	800	5
Palmerston 6i	1560	0.7
Heath TT	950	3
Asquith 380	790	2

1..

2..

3..

4..

Q5 Jo and Brian have fitted both their scooters with the same engine. Brian and his scooter have a combined mass of 110 kg and an acceleration of 2.80 m/s^2. On her scooter, Jo only manages an acceleration of 1.71 m/s^2.

a) What **force** can the engine exert?

....

b) Calculate the combined mass of Jo and her scooter.

....

Q6 Tom drags a 1 kg mass along a table with a newton-meter so that it accelerates at 0.25 m/s^2. If the newton-meter reads 0.4 N, what's the force of friction between the mass and the table?

....

....

....

Q7 A car tows a caravan along a road. At a constant speed, the pulling force of the car and the opposing reaction force of the caravan are equal. Which statement correctly describes the forces between the caravan and the car when the car accelerates? Tick the appropriate box.

☐ "The caravan's reaction force cancels out the pulling force of the car, so the caravan won't accelerate."

☐ "The caravan's reaction force is at a right angle to the force pulling the car, so the two forces don't affect one another."

☐ "The car's pulling force accelerates the caravan. The caravan's reaction acts on the car, not the caravan."

Forces and Acceleration

Q8 Which of the following statements correctly explains what happens when you walk?
Tick the appropriate box.

☐ Your feet push backwards on the ground, so the ground pushes you forwards.

☐ The force in your muscles overcomes the friction between your feet and the ground.

☐ The ground's reaction can't push you backwards because of friction.

☐ Your feet push forwards, and the ground's reaction is upwards.

Q9 A camper van with a mass of 2500 kg has a maximum driving force of 2650 N.
It is driven along a straight, level road at a constant speed of 90 kilometres per hour.
At this speed, air resistance is 2000 N and the friction between the wheel bearings is 500 N.

a) **i)** What force is the engine exerting? ....

ii) Complete the diagram to show all the forces acting on the camper van.
Give the size of each force.

b) A strong headwind begins blowing, with a force of **200 N**. The van slows down.
Calculate its deceleration.

....

c) The driver notices that the van is slowing and puts his foot right down on the accelerator,
applying the maximum driving force. How does the acceleration of the camper van change?
(Assume that air resistance and friction remain at their previous values.)

....

....

....

Top Tips: A resultant force means your object will accelerate — it will change its speed or direction (or both). But if your object has a constant speed (which could be zero) and a constant direction, you can say with utter confidence that there ain't any resultant force. Be careful though — a zero resultant force doesn't mean there are **no** forces, just that they all balance each other out.

Frictional Force and Terminal Velocity

Q1 Use the words supplied to fill in the blanks in the paragraph below about a skydiver. You may need to use some words more than once, or not at all.

decelerates   decrease   less   balances   increase   constant   greater   accelerates

When a skydiver jumps out of a plane, his weight is .... than his air resistance, so he .... downwards. This causes his air resistance to .... until it .... his weight. At this point, his velocity is .... When his parachute opens, his air resistance is .... than his weight, so he .... This causes his air resistance to .... until it .... his weight. Then his velocity is .... once again.

Q2 Which of the following will **reduce** the air resistance force on an aeroplane? Tick any appropriate boxes.

☐ **flying higher (where the air is thinner)**　　☐ **carrying less cargo**

☐ **flying more slowly**　　☐ **making the plane more streamlined**

Q3 A scientist plans to investigate gravity by dropping a hammer and a feather from a tall building. Two onlookers predict what will happen. Say whether each is right or wrong, and explain why.

Paola: "They will land at the same time — gravity is the same for both."

Guiseppe: "The feather will reach its terminal velocity before the hammer."

a) Paola is **right / wrong** because ....
....

b) Guiseppe is **right / wrong** because ....
....

Q4 Mavis is investigating **drag** by dropping balls into a measuring cylinder full of oil and timing how long they take to reach the bottom. She does the experiment with a **golf ball**, a **glass marble** and a **ball bearing**.

From this experiment, can Mavis draw any conclusions about the effect of size on drag? Explain your answer.

....
....

Frictional Force and Terminal Velocity

Q5 The graph shows how the velocity of a skydiver changes before and after he opens his parachute.

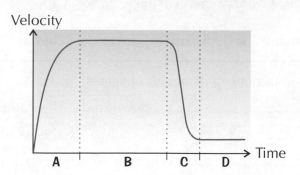

For each of the four regions A-D tick the correct box to say whether the force of **weight** or **air resistance** is greater, or if they are **equal**.

	weight is greater	air resistance is greater	both equal
Region A:	☐	☐	☐
Region B:	☐	☐	☐
Region C:	☐	☐	☐
Region D:	☐	☐	☐

Q6 Two skydivers jump out of a plane. Kate opens her parachute after three seconds, when she is still accelerating rapidly. Alison doesn't open her parachute yet but uses her video camera to film Kate's skydive. On the film Kate's parachute appears to pull her suddenly upwards when it opens.

a) Is Kate really moving upwards? Explain your answer. ....

....

b) Describe how Kate's velocity changes when her parachute opens. ....

....

Q7 On **Venus**, atmospheric pressure is about 90 times that on Earth, but the gravitational field strength is about the same.
On **Mars**, atmospheric pressure is about 1/100th of that on Earth and the gravitational field strength is less than half that on Earth.

Higher atmospheric pressure means the atmosphere is <u>thicker</u> and provides <u>more resistance</u>.

Probes which land on other planets often need parachutes to slow them down during their descent. What **size** of parachute would you recommend, relative to a parachute used on Earth, for:

a) landing on Venus: ....

b) landing on Mars: ....

Top Tips: When objects move through the air at high speed, the air resistance is proportional to the object's **velocity squared**. That's why, for skydivers, air resistance soon balances their weight and they reach terminal velocity. It's also why **driving** very fast is very **inefficient**.

Stopping Distances

Q1 **Stopping distance** and **braking distance** are not the same thing.

a) What is meant by 'braking distance'?

....

b) What is meant by 'thinking distance'?

....

Q2 Will the following factors affect **thinking** distance, **braking** distance or **both**?
Write them in the relevant columns of the table.

tiredness   road surface   weather   speed   drugs

alcohol   tyres   brakes   load

Thinking Distance	Braking Distance

Q3 A car joins a motorway and changes speed from 30 mph to 60 mph.
Which of the following statements are **true**? Tick the appropriate boxes.

☐ The total stopping distance will increase.

☐ The braking force needed to stop in a certain distance will decrease.

☐ Thinking distance will decrease.

☐ Both thinking and braking distance will increase.

Q4 A car has just driven through a deep puddle, making the brakes wet.
Explain why this will increase the stopping distance of the car.

....

....

Q5 Sam is driving when she receives a text message. She decides to try and read it
while still driving. Does this affect her thinking distance? Explain your answer.

....

....

Work and Potential Energy

Q1   Jenny kicks a football, giving it **50 J** of energy.

a)   How much work does Jenny do?

....

b)   If Jenny kicks the ball with a force of **250 N**, over what **distance** does her kick act on the ball?

....

Q2   Explain why pushing your bicycle along a **level** road means that you do some **work** in the scientific sense.

....

....

Q3   Indicate whether the following statements are **true** or **false**.

		True	False
a)	Gravitational potential energy = mass × g × height.	☺	☹
b)	Work done is the energy possessed by an object due to height.	☺	☹
c)	On Earth, the gravitational field strength is approximately **10 N/kg**.	☺	☹
d)	When a force moves an object, work is done.	☺	☹
e)	On Earth, a **3 kg** chicken flies up 2.5 m to sit on a fence. It gains **90 J** of gravitational potential energy.	☺	☹

Q4   Dave works at a DIY shop. He has to load **28** flagstones onto the delivery truck. Each flagstone has a mass of **25 kg** and has to be lifted **1.2 m** onto the truck.

a)   How much gravitational potential energy does one flagstone gain when lifted onto the truck?

....

b)   What is the **total gravitational potential energy** gained by the flagstones after they are all loaded onto the truck?

....

c)   How much **work** does Dave do loading the truck?

....

....

Top Tips: The main thing to remember is that **energy transferred** and **work done** are just the **same** thing. You're bound to get asked to do a calculation, so make sure you know the couple of equations and how to use them. All work questions are pretty similar — so just keep practising and you'll be fine.

Work and Potential Energy

Q5   Shelagh keeps fit by cycling every day. She's calculated that she applies a **steady force** of **50 N** as she cycles. She decides to do at least **80 kJ** of work at each session.

a)   What is the minimum distance Shelagh needs to cycle each session?

....

b) i)   Shelagh unexpectedly comes to a large hill. She does **90 kJ** of work to climb a vertical height of **120 m**. Calculate the size of the force she does work against. Name this force.

....

....

ii)   Calculate the combined mass of Shelagh and her bike.

....

Q6   Jo is sitting at the top of a helter-skelter ride and her mass is **50 kg**.

a)   If her gravitational potential energy is **4000 J**, how high up is Jo?

....

b)   She comes down the helter-skelter and at the bottom her kinetic energy is **1500 J**. How much **energy** has been 'wasted' coming down the ride?

....

c)   Which **force** causes this energy to be wasted? ....

d)   If the ride is **50 m** long, what is the average energy-wasting force?

....

e)   Jo has another go on the helter-skelter but this time she slides down on a mat. At the bottom of the ride, her kinetic energy is **2000 J**. What is the average energy-wasting **force** on this turn on the ride?

....

....

f)   Explain why Jo has a **different** kinetic energy at the bottom when she slides down on a mat.

....

g)   At the bottom of the ride Jo and the mat take a distance of **5 m** to stop. What is the average stopping **force**?

....

....

Kinetic Energy

Q1 Decide if the following statements are **true** or **false**.

		True	False
a)	Kinetic energy is energy due to movement.	☺	☹
b)	Heat from the Sun causes space shuttles to heat up as they re-enter the atmosphere.	☺	☹
c)	Friction between meteors and the atmosphere causes most meteors to burn up before they reach the Earth.	☺	☹

Q2 A toy cricket ball hit straight upwards has a gravitational potential energy of **242 J** at the **top** of its flight.

a) What is the ball's **kinetic energy just** before it hits the ground?

....

b) Calculate the speed of the ball at this time if its mass is **100 g**.

....

Q3 A large truck and a car both have a kinetic energy of **614 400 J**. The mass of the truck is **12 288 kg** and the car **1200 kg**.

a) Calculate the **speed** of:

i) the car ....

ii) the truck ....

b) John is playing with his remote-controlled toy car and truck. The car's mass is 100 g. The truck's mass is 300 g. The car is moving twice as fast as the truck. Which has more kinetic energy — the car or the truck? Explain your answer.

....

....

Q4 Jack rides his bicycle along a level road and has a total kinetic energy of **1440 J**. He brakes, exerting a force of **200 N** on the wheels.

a) How far does he travel before he stops?

....

b) What happens to the temperature of the brakes? Explain your answer.

....

> ### Top Tips:
> It's all about moving — the bigger the mass and the faster something moves the larger its kinetic energy. Get friendly with that formula — it crops up everywhere.

Forces and Elasticity

Q1 Alice is bouncing on a trampoline. Springs around the edge hold the trampoline bed in place.

a) The springs that hold the trampoline bed are **elastic objects**. Describe what 'elastic' means.

....

b) When she is at the top of a bounce Alice has **gravitational potential energy**. This is transferred to **kinetic energy** as she falls back down, but at the bottom of the bounce the kinetic energy is **zero**. Explain what happens to her kinetic energy.

....

....

c) Alice exerts a force of 600 N on the trampoline at the bottom of her bounce

i) There are 30 springs that support the trampoline bed. Calculate the **force exerted per spring**. Assume that **only the springs extend**, and that this force is **evenly spread** across the springs.

....

ii) An individual spring extends by **10 cm** at the bottom of a bounce. Calculate its **spring constant**.

....

....

Q2 Nick the bungee jumper is checking his bungee cords.

a) One cord has a spring constant **45 N/m**. Calculate how much force is required to stretch it by **15 m**.

....

b) Nick conducts an experiment to find how much force it takes to stretch the bungee rope by different amounts. His results are plotted on the graph below and a best fit line is drawn.

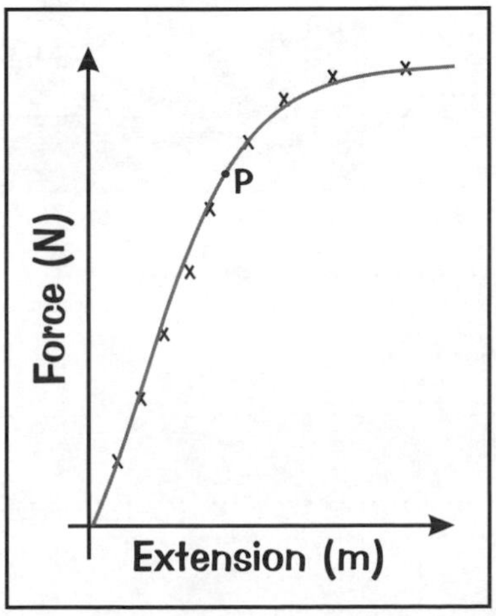

i) Name the point labelled **P**.

....

ii) Nick repeats his experiment with the **same bungee cord** and plots the results in a graph. Will he get an identical force-extension curve? Explain your answer.

....

....

....

Power

Q1 Complete this passage by using the words provided.

heat	energy	one hundred	rate	light	watts	joules

Power is the .... of doing work, or how much .... is

transferred per second. It is measured in .... or ....

per second. A 100 W light bulb transfers .... joules of electrical

energy into .... and .... each second.

Q2 George drives to work every day in a small car with a **power** output of **50 kW**.

a) Write down an equation that relates **power** to **energy**.

....

b) If the journey takes **5 minutes**, how much **energy** does the car get from its fuel?

....

c) One day George's car breaks down and so he cycles to work. The journey takes him **12 minutes** and he uses **144 kJ** of energy. How much **power** does he generate?

....

Q3 Catherine and Sally decide to run up a set of stairs to see who can get to the top more quickly. Catherine has a mass of **46 kg** and Sally has a mass of **48 kg**. $g = 10 \, N/kg$

a) The top of the stairs is **5 m** above ground.
Calculate the gain in **potential energy** for:

i) Catherine

....

ii) Sally

....

b) Catherine won the race in **6.2 s**, while Sally took **6.4 s**.
Which girl generated more **power**?

....

....

Power

Q4 Tom likes to build model boats. His favourite boat is the Carter, which has a motor power of **150 W**.

a) How much **energy** does the Carter transfer in **10 minutes**?

....

b) The petrol for the boat's motor can supply **30 kJ/ml**. What volume of petrol is used up in **10 minutes**?

....

c) Tom decides to get a model speed boat which transfers **120 kJ** in the same 10 minute journey. What is the **power** of the engine?

....

Q5 Josie runs home after school so she can watch her favourite TV programme. She has a mass of **60 kg** and her school bag has a mass of **6 kg**.

a) At the start of her run, she accelerates steadily from **0** to **8 m/s** in **6 seconds** while carrying her bag. Calculate her power for this part of her run.

....

b) Josie gets to her house, she puts **down** her school bag, and then runs up the stairs to her room. It takes her **4 seconds** to get to the top of the stairs, where she is **5 m** above ground level. How much power does she generate getting up the stairs?

....

Q6 Andy loves running and wants to improve his starts in sprint races. He uses a timing gate to measure his maximum speed and how long the start takes him. He has a mass of **70 kg**.

Sprint number	Time taken (s)	Maximum speed (m/s)
1	3.2	8.0
2	3.1	8.2
3	3.3	7.9
4 *	4.6	7.2
5	3.2	7.9

*He slips at the start because his shoes don't grip properly.

a) Andy records data for five starts as shown. Which start data set should be ignored?

....

b) Calculate the average **time** taken and the average **speed** achieved in the reliable starts.

....

....

c) What is Andy's average **power** over the reliable starts?

....

Momentum and Collisions

Q1 Circle the correct words or phrases to make the following statements true.

a) If the velocity of a moving object doubles, its **kinetic energy** / **momentum** will double.

b) If you drop a suitcase out of a moving car, the car's momentum will **decrease** / **increase**.

c) When two objects collide the total momentum **changes** / **stays the same**.

d) When a force acts on an object its momentum **changes** / **stays the same**.

Q2 Place the following four trucks in order of increasing momentum.

Truck A
speed = 30 m/s
mass = 3000 kg

Truck B
speed = 10 m/s
mass = 4500 kg

Truck C
speed = 20 m/s
mass = 4000 kg

Truck D
speed = 15 m/s
mass = 3500 kg

....

....

....

(lowest momentum)   .... , ... , ... , ...   (highest momentum)

Q3 Shopping trolley A has a mass of 10 kg and is moving east at 4 m/s. It collides with trolley B which has a mass of 30 kg and is moving west at 1 m/s. The two trolleys join together.

a) Complete the diagram showing the masses and velocities of the trolleys **before** they collide.

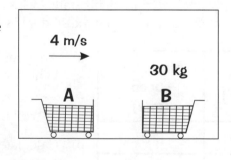

For this one you'll need to know the total momentum of the two trolleys before the collision.

b) Find the **velocity** of the trolleys **after** the collision (when they are joined) and draw a diagram showing their speed and direction.

....

....

....

....

Physics 2a — Motion, Energy and Electricity

Car Design and Safety

Q1   Use the words in the box to fill in the gaps in the paragraph below.

electric generator	reverse	heat	chemical
efficient		work	regenerative

When the brakes of a car are applied, they do .... on the

wheels, transferring kinetic energy into .... and sound

energy. New .... braking systems put the vehicle's motor

into .... to slow the wheels down.

The motor works as an .... and converts the kinetic

energy of the wheels into electrical energy. This can then be used to charge

the vehicle's battery — storing the electrical energy as ....

energy. By finding a use for this previously 'wasted' energy, these new braking

systems make cars more ....

Q2   A car travels along a level road and brakes to avoid hitting a cat.

a)   What type of **energy** does the moving car have?

....

b)   Explain how energy is **conserved** as the brakes slow down the car.

....

....

Q3   Clive's car has a top speed of 150 mph. He attaches a roof box to his car. How will this affect its top speed? Explain your answer.

....

....

....

Car Design and Safety

Q4   Modern cars are now fitted with many **safety features**, including seat belts.

a)   Explain why car safety features are designed to **slow** the car and its occupants down over the **longest** possible time in a collision.

....

....

b)   State **two other** safety features which increase the time taken for passengers to slow down in a crash. For each feature, explain **how** it helps to convert **kinetic energy** more safely.

....

....

....

....

Q5   Since 1991 it has been compulsory in the UK for all adults to wear seat belts in both the front and back seats of a car.

a)   Explain how a seat belt **absorbs** energy to slow down a passenger when a crash occurs.

....

b)   Explain, in terms of **momentum changes**, how this protects the passenger's internal organs.

....

....

....

Q6   A sports car transfers **2 650 000 kJ** of chemical energy **per hour** into kinetic energy. Calculate its power output.

$power = energy \div time$

....

....

....

Top Tips: In a car crash there's a sudden change in velocity, which means a sudden change in momentum. To help protect the passengers inside, the car needs to make the momentum change more slowly — if you're in a serious crash you want the car to be the one all crumpled up, not you.

Static Electricity

Q1 **Circle** the pairs of charges that would attract each other and **underline** those that would repel.

positive and positive   positive and negative   negative and positive   negative and negative

Q2 Fill in the gaps in these sentences with the words below.

electrons	positive	static	friction	insulating	negative

.... electricity can build up when two .... materials

are rubbed together. The .... moves .... from one

material onto the other. This leaves a .... charge on one of the

materials and a .... charge on the other.

Q3 The sentences below are wrong. Write out a **correct** version for each.

a) A polythene rod becomes negatively charged when rubbed with a duster because it loses electrons.

....

....

b) When a negatively charged object and a positively charged object are brought together, only the negative object exerts a force.

....

....

c) The closer two charged objects are together, the less strongly they attract or repel.

....

....

d) Electrical charges can't move very easily through metals.

....

....

Q4 Russell hates his jumper. Whenever he takes it off his hair stands on end. Explain why this happens.

....

....

Current and Potential Difference

Q1 Use the words below to complete the passage.

reduces	voltage	decrease	charge	work

Electric current is the flow of electric .... around a circuit. Current flows

through a component which has a potential difference (................................) across it.

The potential difference between two points in an circuit is the .... done per

coulomb of charge that passes between the points. Resistance .... the flow

of current — to increase the current in a circuit you can .... the resistance.

Q2 Connect the quantities with their units and their symbols.

 A  Current volts

V Resistance amps

Ω Potential Difference ohms

Q3 A 3 volt battery can supply a current of 5 amps for 20 minutes before it needs recharging.

a) Calculate how much charge the battery can provide before it needs recharging.

....

Tip: convert to seconds first.

....

b) Each coulomb of charge from the battery can carry 3 J of energy.
Calculate how much work the battery can do before it needs recharging.

....

Q4 Sally is comparing two lamps, A and B. She takes the measurements shown in the table.

Calculate the **missing values**
and write them in the table.

	Lamp A	Lamp B
Current through lamp (A)	2	4
Potential difference across lamp (V)	3	2
Charge passing in 10 s (C)		
Work done in 10 s (J)		

Q5 The motor in a fan is attached to a 9 V battery.
If a current of 4 A flows through the motor for 7 minutes:

a) Calculate the total charge passed.

....

b) Calculate the work done by the motor.

....

Circuits — The Basics

Q1   Match up these items from a standard test circuit with the **correct description** and **symbol**.

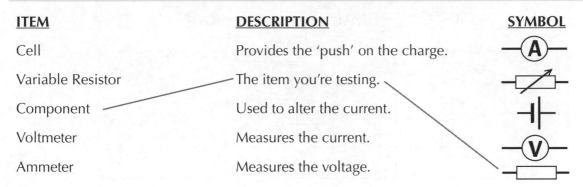

ITEM	DESCRIPTION	SYMBOL
Cell	Provides the 'push' on the charge.	—Ⓐ—
Variable Resistor	The item you're testing.	
Component	Used to alter the current.	—‖—
Voltmeter	Measures the current.	—Ⓥ—
Ammeter	Measures the voltage.	

Q2   Complete the following passage by using the words from the box.

circuit	across	through

You can measure the resistance of a component using a standard test

.... To work out the resistance of the component, you need to

measure the current .... the component using an ammeter

and the potential difference .... it using a voltmeter.

Q3   The diagram below shows a **complete circuit**.

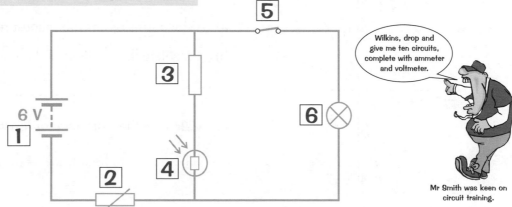

Wilkins, drop and give me ten circuits, complete with ammeter and voltmeter.

Mr Smith was keen on circuit training.

a)   Give the name of each of the numbered components.

1. ....   2. ....

3. ....   4. ....

5. ....   6. ....

b)   Draw an **ammeter** on the circuit in the correct position to measure the current leaving the battery.

c)   Draw a **voltmeter** on the circuit in the correct position to measure the voltage across the lamp.

Resistance and V = I × R

Q1 Match the correct label to each of the **V-I graphs** below.

RESISTOR   FILAMENT LAMP   DIODE

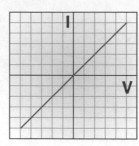

A ....   B ....   C ....

Q2 Indicate whether the following are **true** or **false**.

	True	False
a) The resistance of a filament lamp falls as the temperature of the filament increases.	☐	☐
b) The steeper the gradient of a V-I graph, the lower the resistance.	☐	☐
c) Current can flow freely through a diode in both directions.	☐	☐
d) The current through a resistor at constant temperature is proportional to the voltage.	☐	☐
e) Current can flow both ways through a lamp.	☐	☐

Q3 The graph below shows V-I curves for four resistors.

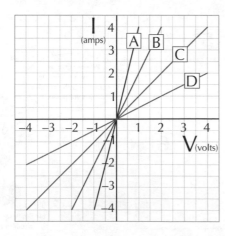

Gradient = $\dfrac{\text{vertical change}}{\text{horizontal change}}$

a) Which resistor has the highest resistance? ....

b) Calculate the gradient of the line for resistor B.

....

c) Calculate the resistance of resistor B.

....

Q4 An electrical current flowing through a **filament bulb** causes it to get **hot**. Explain why this makes its resistance **increase**. You should give your answer in terms of **electrons** and **ions**.

....

....

....

....

Resistance and V = I × R

Q5 Fill in the missing values in the table below.

Use the formula triangle to help.

Voltage (V)	Current (A)	Resistance (Ω)
6	2	
8		2
	3	3
4	8	
2		4
	0.5	2

Q6 Peter tested **three components** using a standard test circuit. The table below shows his results.

Voltage (V)	−4.0	3.0	−2.0	−1.0	0.0	1.0	2.0	3.0	4.0
Component **A** current (A)	−2.0	−1.5	−1.0	−0.5	0.0	0.5	1.0	1.5	2.0
Component **B** current (A)	0.0	0.0	0.0	0.0	0.0	0.2	1.0	2.0	4.5
Component **C** current (A)	−4.0	−3.5	−3.0	−2.0	0.0	2.0	3.0	3.5	4.0

a) Draw a **V-I graph** for each component on the axes below.

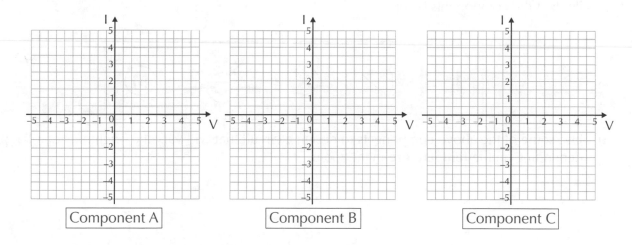

Component A   Component B   Component C

b) Complete Peter's **conclusions**:

Component **A** is a ....

Component **B** is a ....

Component **C** is a ....

___

Top Tips: There are two very important skills you need to master for resistance questions —
interpreting V-I graphs and using the formula **V = I × R**. Make sure you can do both.

Circuit Devices

Q1 Use the words below to fill in the gaps. You won't need to use all the words.

light-dependent	lights	thermistor	vary	thermostats	diode

The resistance of some components can .... The resistance of a

.... goes up as the temperature decreases — this makes them useful as

electronic .... The resistance of a .... resistor

depends on the intensity of light falling on it — its resistance drops when light shines on it.

They're often used to automatically switch on .... when it gets dark.

Q2 **LEDs** are used in electrical appliances and for lighting.

a) Briefly describe how an LED works.

....

b) Suggest **one** reason why there is an increasing use of LEDs as lighting.

....

....

Q3 Look at the components below.

a) Use **some** of the above components to design a circuit that will vary the brightness of a **lamp**, depending on the **temperature** in the room.

b) What happens to the **resistance** in the circuit as the room temperature **increases**?

....

c) What happens to the **brightness** of the lamp as the room temperature **decreases**?

....

Series Circuits

Q1   Match up these definitions with what they describe in a series circuit.

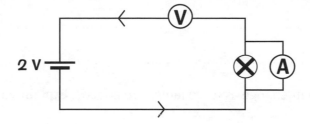

Same everywhere in the circuit

Shared by all the components

The sum of the resistances

Can be different for each component

Potential difference

Current

Total potential difference

Total resistance

Q2   Eva has drawn a series circuit she plans to set up, but she's made **three** mistakes.

a)   List Eva's mistakes.

1. ....

2. ....

3. ....

b)   In the space to the right, **redraw** the circuit with the mistakes corrected.

Q3   The diagram shows a series circuit.

a)   Calculate the total potential difference across the battery.

....

b)   Work out the total resistance.

....

c)   Calculate the resistance of resistor R_3.

....

d)   What would you expect the reading on the voltmeter to be?

....

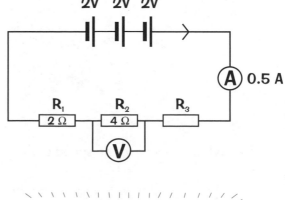

For parts b) and d), you'll need to use the formula connecting V, I and R.

Series Circuits

Q4 Vikram does an experiment with different numbers of lamps in a series circuit. The diagram below shows his three circuits.

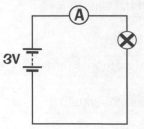 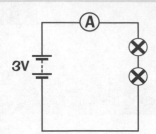 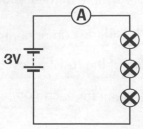 

a) What do you think happens to the **brightness** of the lamps as he adds more of them? **Explain** your answer.

....

....

b) How does the **current** change as more lamps are added? **Explain** your answer.

....

....

Q5 Here are some instructions for making a series circuit that will **vary the speed of a motor**:

> Connect the following in series...
>
> Two batteries — 3 V each
> Variable resistor
> Ammeter
> Motor of resistance 2 Ω (symbol (M))

a) Use the instructions to **draw** the circuit.

b) What happens to the **speed** of the motor as the resistance of the variable resistor is increased?

....

c) Calculate the **current** in the circuit when the resistance of the variable resistor is **1 Ω**.

....

....

Parallel Circuits

Q1 Tick to show whether these statements about parallel circuits are **true** or **false**.

		True	False
a)	Components are connected side-by-side (instead of end-to-end).	☐	☐
b)	Each component has the same potential difference across it.	☐	☐
c)	The current is the same everywhere in the circuit.	☐	☐
d)	Components can be switched on and off independently.	☐	☐

Q2 The diagrams show currents at junctions in two parallel circuits.

Write in the **missing** values.

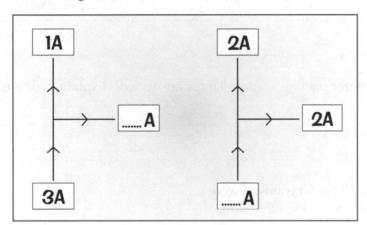

Q3 Find the **missing values** in this parallel circuit.

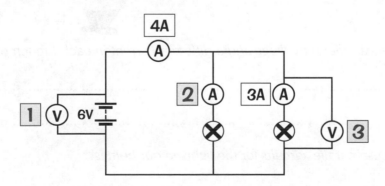

1. ....

2. ....

3. ....

Parallel Circuits

Q4   Karen does an experiment with different numbers of lamps
in a parallel circuit. The diagrams below show her three circuits.

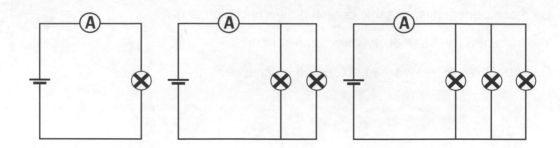

a)   What happens to the **brightness** of the lamps as Karen adds more of them? **Explain** your answer.

....

....

b)   What happens to the **ammeter** reading as more lamps are added? **Explain** your answer.

....

....

c)   One of the lamps in the third circuit is **unscrewed**.
What happens to the brightness of the other lamps?

....

Q5   Answer Shane's questions about parallel circuits.
Make sure you explain your answers.

a)   *"Can you have a different voltage and a different current in each branch of the circuit?"*

....

....

b)   *"Why do we use parallel circuits for the lights in our homes?"*

....

....

Top Tips: It's really important you know the differences between series and parallel circuits.
Make sure you understand what happens to the current and voltage across components in both types.

Physics 2a — Motion, Energy and Electricity

Series and Parallel Circuits — Examples

Q1   **Complete** this table for series and parallel circuits:

	SERIES CIRCUITS	PARALLEL CIRCUITS
Components connected	end to end	
Current		can be different in each branch
Voltage	shared between components	
Example of use		

Q2   A set of **Christmas tree lights** is designed to work on mains voltage (230 V). It has **12 V** bulbs.

a)   How can you tell that these lights are wired in series?

....

....

b)   Why might it be better to wire Christmas tree lights in **parallel**?

....

....

c)   Give one reason why you can't usually swap bulbs between series and parallel sets of lights.

....

....

Q3   Fill in the **four** missing values on this **series** circuit:

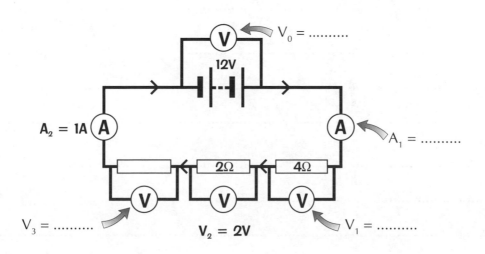

Series and Parallel Circuits — Examples

Q4 The diagram opposite shows a **parallel** circuit.

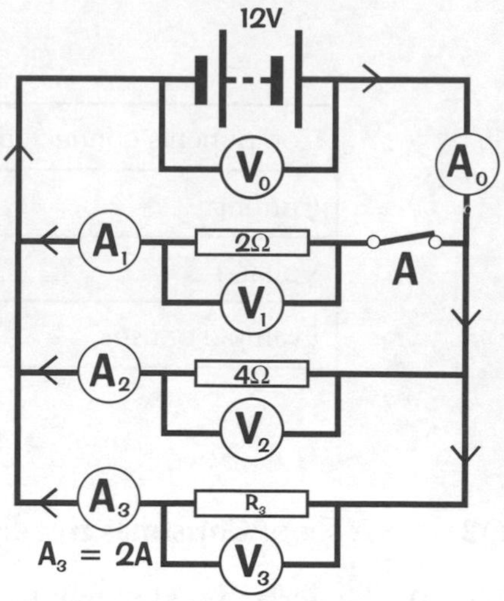

a) Calculate the readings on ammeters:

  i) A_1 ....

  ii) A_2 ....

b) Find the readings on voltmeters:

  i) V_1 ....

  ii) V_2 ....

c) What is the reading on ammeter A_0 when switch A is open?

  ....

  ....

Q5 A group of pupils make the following **observations**:

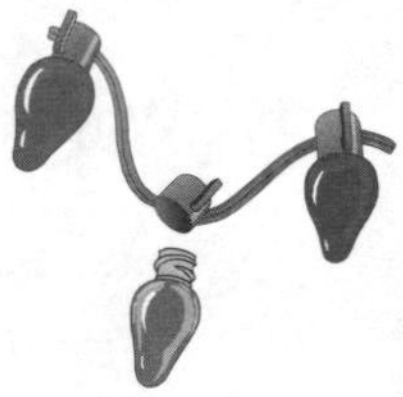

  1. "The lights go dim if you switch the fan on in a parked car."

  2. "You can switch Christmas tree lights off by unscrewing one of the bulbs."

  3. "The lights in my house are wired in parallel, but all the wall lights in the living room go on and off together."

Explain their observations.

1. ....

  ....

  ....

2. ....

  ....

  ....

3. ....

  Think about what makes them go on and off.

  ....

  ....

  ....

Physics 2a — Motion, Energy and Electricity

Mixed Questions — Physics 2a

Q1 Mr Alonso drives his car at a constant speed for **1500 m**. The engine produces a force of **300 N**.

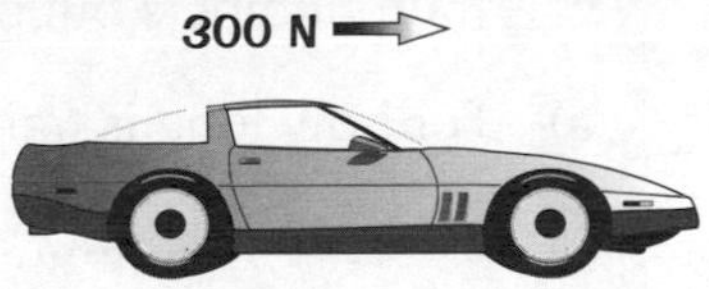

300 N ➡

a) How much work does the engine do?

....

b) Mr. Alonso then accelerates, increasing his speed by 20 m/s over 6.2 s. Calculate his acceleration.

....

c) As it's a hot day, Mr. Alonso winds down his windows.
Explain how and why this will alter the **top speed** of the car.

....

....

d) Explain how wearing a seat belt will keep Mr. Alonso safer in a crash.

....

Q2 Jack and Jill go up a hill to go on a roller coaster. With them in it, the roller coaster carriage has a total mass of **1200 kg**.

a) At the start of the ride the carriage rises up to its highest point of **34 m** above the ground and stops. Calculate its gain in gravitational potential energy.

....

b) The carriage then falls to a third of its maximum height. Assuming there is no air resistance or friction, calculate the speed of the carriage at this point.

....

....

c) At the end of the ride, the carriage slows down, decelerating at **6.4 m/s²**.
How long does it take the carriage to slow down from 20 m/s and come to a stop?

....

Q3 The diagram shows a circuit in which three resistors are connected in series.

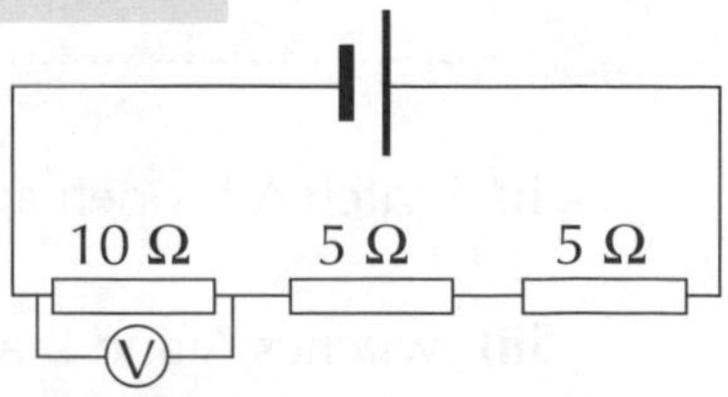

a) Calculate the total resistance of the 3 resistors.

....

$10\,\Omega$ $5\,\Omega$ $5\,\Omega$

b) If the voltmeter shown reads 4 V, find:

i) the current flowing in the circuit. ....

ii) the voltage of the power supply. ....

....

Physics 2a — Motion, Energy and Electricity

Mixed Questions — Physics 2a

Q4 Norman loves trainspotting. As a special treat, he not only notes the train numbers but plots a **distance-time** graph for two of the trains.

a) For how long is train 2 stationary?

....

b) Calculate the initial speed of the faster train.

....

c) Describe the motion of train 1 between 40 s and 80 s.

....

Q5 Cherie and Tony rob a bank. They escape in a getaway car with a mass of **2100 kg** and travel at a constant speed of **90 km/h** along a straight, level road.

a) Is there a resultant force on the car? Explain your answer.

....

b) Calculate the momentum of the car.

....

c) A police car swings into the middle of the road and stops ahead of Cherie's car. Cherie slams on the brakes. The car comes to a halt **3.0 s** after she hits the brakes.

i) Write down **one** factor that could affect Cherie's thinking distance.

....

ii) Assuming the car decelerates uniformly, find the force acting on the braking car.

....

Q6 The diagram shows a circuit which could be used for the lights on a car. Each headlight bulb is rated at 12 V, 6 A and each side light bulb is rated at 12 V, 0.5 A.

a) Calculate the total current flowing from the battery if:

i) Switch A is closed and switch B is open.

....

ii) Switch A is open and switch B is closed. ....

iii) Switches A and B are both closed. ....

b) The car has a **thermostat** to regulate temperature in the engine. Name the **type** of resistor used in a thermostat and briefly **describe** how this type of resistor works.

....

Mixed Questions — Physics 2a

Q7 In the film 'Crouching Sparrow, Hidden Beaver', a **95 kg** dummy is dropped **60 m** from the top of a building. (Assume that g = 10 m/s².)

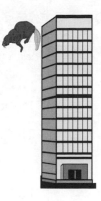

a) Sketch a distance-time graph and a velocity-time graph for the dummy from the moment it is dropped until just after it hits the ground. (Ignore air resistance and assume the dummy does not reach a terminal speed.)

b) The take doesn't go to plan so the dummy is lifted back to the top of the building using a motor.

   i) How much work is done on the dummy to get it to the top of the building?

   ....

   ii) The useful power output of the motor is **760 W**.
   How long does it take to get the dummy to the top of the building?

   ....

c) The dummy is getting a bit damaged, being dropped repeatedly, so an elastic cord is attached to it. Calculate the **spring constant** of the cord if it stretches by **5 m** when the dummy is hanging on the end.

....

Q8 A sky-diver jumps out of an aeroplane. Her weight is **700 N**.

a) What force causes her to accelerate downwards?

....

b) After **10 s** she is falling at a steady speed of **60 m/s**.
State the force of air resistance that is acting on her.

....

c) She now opens her parachute, which increases the air resistance to **2000 N**.
Explain what happens immediately after she opens the parachute.

....

....

d) After falling with her parachute open for **5 s**, the sky-diver is travelling at a steady speed of **4 m/s**.
What is the air resistance force now?

....

Mains Electricity

Q1 Choose from the words below to fill in the gaps.

| changing | batteries | hertz | d.c. | volts | direct |
| alternating | a.c. | same | frequency | amps | direction |

In the United Kingdom the mains electrical supply is about 230 ....

The supply is .... current (..............) which means that the

.... of the current is constantly .... The supply

has a .... of 50 cycles per second (50 ....).

Cells and .... supply .... current (................) —

the current always passes in the .... direction.

Q2 The diagram shows three traces on the same CRO. The settings are the same in each case.

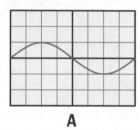 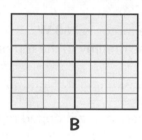 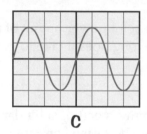

A   B   C

Write down the **letter** of the trace that shows:

a) the highest frequency a.c. ....,   **b)** direct current ....,   **c)** the lowest a.c. voltage ....

Q3 The diagram shows a trace on a CRO screen.
The **timebase** is set to 10 ms per division,
and the **gain** to 1 volt per division.

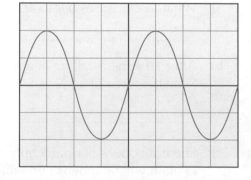

a) What is the peak voltage? ....

b) What is the time period?

....

....

c) Calculate the frequency of the supply.

....

....

Top Tips: Knowing the difference between a.c. and d.c. isn't too tricky, it's knowing how to work out stuff like the potential difference from a CRO screen that's the hard bit. Learn it all, folks.

Electricity in the Home

Q1 Look at this picture of a kitchen. Put a **ring** round everything that is **unsafe**.

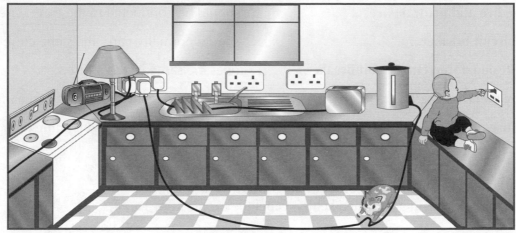

Q2 Answer the following questions about **plugs**:

a) Why is the body of a plug made of rubber or plastic?

....

b) Explain why some parts of a plug are made from copper or brass.

....

c) What material is the cable insulation made from, and why?

....

Q3 Use the words below to complete these rules for wiring a plug.

outer   bare   live   earth   neutral   insulation   firmly   green and yellow

a) Strip the .... off the end of each wire.

b) Connect the brown wire to the .... terminal.

c) Connect the blue wire to the .... terminal.

d) Connect the .... wire to the .... terminal.

e) Check all the wires are .... screwed in with no .... bits showing.

f) The cable grip must be securely fastened over the .... covering of the cable.

Q4 This plug is **incorrectly** wired. Write down the **three** mistakes.

	= Neutral
	= Live
	= Earth

1. ....

2. ....

3. ....

Fuses and Earthing

Q1   **Match** up the beginnings and endings of these sentences:

The live and neutral wires...	... should be connected to the earth wire.
A circuit breaker...	... should normally carry the same current.
A Residual Current Circuit Breaker...	... does the same job as a fuse.
Any metal casing...	... can be used instead of a fuse and earth wire.
A fuse melts when the current...	... in a fuse wire exceeds the rating of the fuse.

Q2   Put these events in the correct order to describe what happens when a fault occurs in an earthed kettle. Label the events from 1 to 4.

☐ The device is isolated from the live wire.   ☐ A big current flows out through the earth wire.

☐ A big surge in current blows the fuse.   ☐ A fault allows the live wire to touch the metal case.

Q3   Some circuits are protected by Residual Current Circuit breakers (RCCBs).

a)   Briefly describe how an RCCB works.

....

....

b)   Give two advantages of using RCCBs instead of fuses.

1. ....

2. ....

Q4   A 'double insulated' hair dryer uses a current of 0.25 A.

a)   Andrea has fuses rated 0.25 A, 2 A and 8 A.
Which fuse should she fit in the plug for the hair dryer?   ....

b)   Why does the hair dryer **not** need an **earth wire**?

....

c)   What type of electrical cable will the hair dryer have? Circle the correct answer.

two-core cable   three-core cable

d)   Andrea notices the electrical supply cable for her TV is much thicker than for her hair dryer. Explain how **cable thickness** and **fuse ratings** of appliances are **linked**.

....

....

Energy and Power in Circuits

Q1 Fill in the gaps using the words in the box.

power	energy	more	heat	how long	time

The energy transferred by an appliance depends on .... it's used

for and its .... The power of an appliance can be calculated

using the formula: power = ... ÷ ....

Whenever an electrical current flows through anything with an electrical resistance,

electrical energy is converted into .... energy. The less energy

wasted, e.g. as heat by an appliance, the .... efficient it is.

Q2 Raj is comparing **three** different types of light bulb. Below is a summary of his findings.

	Fluorescent bulb	Light-emitting diode (LED) bulb	Filament bulb
Energy efficiency	~10%	~75%	~2%
Cost	£3.50	£25	50p

a) Suggest **one** reason why the filament bulb has a low efficiency.

....

b) Give **one** reason why Raj might choose to buy the **LED** bulb rather than the other two types.

....

c) Suggest why Raj might choose to buy the filament bulb rather than the other two types.

....

....

Q3 Calculate the **amount** of electrical energy used by the following.
For each component, say what **forms** of energy the electrical energy is converted to.

a) A 100 watt lamp in 10 seconds: .... J.

Electrical energy is converted to .... and .... energy.

b) A 500 watt motor in 2 minutes: .... J.

Electrical energy is converted to ...., ... and .... energy.

c) A 1 kW heater in 20 seconds: .... J.

Electrical energy is converted to .... energy.

d) A 2 kW heater in 10 minutes: .... J.

Electrical energy is converted to .... energy.

Remember to put time in seconds and power in W.

Physics 2b — Electricity and the Atom

Power and Energy Change

Q1 Lucy is comparing **three lamps**. She connects each lamp in a circuit and measures the **current**. Her results are shown in the table below.

	Lamp A	Lamp B	Lamp C
Voltage (V)	12	3	230
Current (A)	2.5	4	0.1
Power (W)			
Energy used in one minute (J)			

a) Complete the table by filling in the missing values.

b) What rating of fuse would each lamp need?

   A = ...,   B = ...,   C = ...

Typical fuse ratings are 1, 2, 3, 5, 7, 10 or 13A.

Q2 An electric heater is rated at **230 V, 1500 W**.

a) Calculate the current it uses.

....

....

b) What rating of fuse should be used with this heater? Circle your choice.

   1 A   **2 A**   **3 A**   **5 A**   **7 A**   **10 A**   **13 A**

Q3 Henry is comparing two electric drills. He takes the measurements shown in the table below. Calculate the **missing values** and write them in the table.

	Drill A	Drill B
Current through drill (A)	2	3
Voltage drop across drill (V)	230	230
Charge passing in 5 s (C)		
Energy transformed in 5 s (J)		

Remember, current = charge ÷ time.

Q4 Tim's toy boat has a motor attached to a **2 V** battery. A current of **0.6 A** runs through the boat when it's switched on. Tim turns his boat on and leaves it running in his bath for **12 minutes**.

a) Calculate the total charge passed.

....

b) Calculate the energy transformed by the motor.

....

Atomic Structure

Q1   **Complete** the following sentences.

a)   Neutral atoms have .... charge.

b)   A charged atom is called an ....

c)   A neutral atom has the same number of .... and ....

d)   If an electron is removed from a neutral atom, the atom becomes .... charged.

Q2   **Complete** this table.

Particle	Mass	Charge
Proton	1	
	1	0
Electron		−1

Q3   In the early 1900s, the '**plum pudding**' model of the atom was replaced by **Rutherford** and **Marsden's** nuclear model.

a)   i)   Briefly describe the **experiment** Rutherford and Marsden carried out.

....

....

ii)   What did they **expect** to happen in the experiment?

....

....

b)   Rutherford and Marsden used the results from their experiments to disprove the **plum pudding model** and come up with the **nuclear model** of the atom. Describe the **results** of their experiment, and what they showed about the **structure of the atom**.

....

....

....

....

....

....

I'm a swimwear model.

Top Tips: Make sure you can explain how the results from Rutherford and Marsden's scattering experiments led to the 'plum pudding' model being replaced by the nuclear model of the atom.

Atoms and Ionising Radiation

Q1   Indicate whether these sentences are **true** or **false**.

                                                                        True False

a)   The total number of neutrons in an atom is called the atomic number.   ☐ ☐

b)   The total number of protons and neutrons in an atom is called the mass number.   ☐ ☐

c)   Atoms of the same element with the same number of neutrons are called isotopes.   ☐ ☐

d)   Radioactive decay speeds up at higher temperatures.   ☐ ☐

e)   Radioactive decay is a random process — you can't predict when it will happen.   ☐ ☐

Q2   **Radiation doses** are measured in **Sieverts (Sv)**.

a)   While you are reading this you are receiving about 2 mSv/year.

    i) What is causing this?

    ....

    ii) Suggest two **man-made** sources that might contribute to this radiation.

       1. ....

       2. ....

b)   The table below shows some typical radiation doses.

	Dose in Sv
50% survival probability, whole body dose	4 (single dose)
Legal worker dose limit (whole body)	0.02 per year
Average dose from all sources in Cornwall	0.008 per year
Average dose from natural radiation	0.002 per year
Average dose from a UK to Spain flight	0.00001 (single dose)

    i) Suggest why people living in Cornwall have a higher than normal dose.

    ....

    ii) Give **one** other natural source of background radiation.

    ....

    iii) A British pilot flies to Spain **and back** 500 times per year. If he
        lives in Cornwall, is his annual dose below the legal worker limit?

    ....

Atoms and Ionising Radiation

Q3 Match up each description with the correct type of radiation.

Alpha particle   2 neutrons and 2 protons — the same as a helium nucleus.

Beta particle   A type of electromagnetic radiation.

Gamma radiation   An electron from the nucleus.

Q4 Complete the table below by choosing the correct word from each column.

Radiation Type	Ionising power weak/ moderate/ strong	Charge positive/ none/ negative	Relative mass no mass/ small/large	Penetrating power low/moderate/ high	Range in air short/long/ very long
alpha					
beta					
gamma					

Q5 Write the nuclear equations for the following decay processes.

a) An atom of thorium-234 ($^{234}_{90}$Th) emits a beta particle and becomes an atom of protactinium (Pa).

....

b) An atom of radon-222 ($^{222}_{86}$Rn) emits an alpha particle and becomes an atom of polonium (Po).

....

Q6 The diagram to the right shows the paths of an alpha particle and beta particle in an **electric field**.

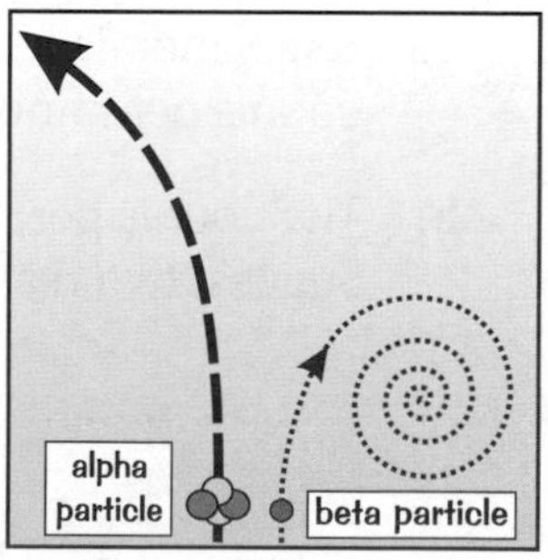

Identify **two** ways in which the path of the alpha and beta particle differ and **explain** the reason for each difference.

1. ....

....

....

2. ....

....

Physics 2b — Electricity and the Atom

Half-Life

Q1   A radioactive isotope has a half-life of **60 years**.
Which of these statements describes this isotope correctly? Tick one box only.

In 60 years, half of the atoms in the material will have gone. ☐

In 30 years' time, only half the atoms will be radioactive. ☐

In 60 years' time, the count rate will be half what it is now. ☐

In about 180 years there will be almost no radioactivity left in the material. ☐

Q2   The half-life of strontium-90 is **29 years**.

a)   What does this tell you will have happened to a pure sample of strontium-90 in 29 years' time?

....

b)   If you start with 1000 atoms of strontium-90, how many would you expect there to be after 87 years?

....

Q3   The activity of a radioactive sample is **1440 cpm**. 5 hours later
it has fallen to **45 cpm**. What is the half-life of this material?

....

....

Q4   Sandra measures how the radioactivity of a sample changes with time.
The table shows some of her results.

Time (minutes)	0	10	20	30	40	80	160
Counts per minute	740	553	420	326	260	140	103

a)   Use Sandra's results to draw a graph of
counts per minute against time.

b)   The counts per minute will never fall below 100.
Suggest two reasons why.

....

....

c)   Sandra calculates that the half-life of her sample is
about 20 minutes. Explain how she worked this out.
(You may find it useful to show some of the working on your graph.)

....

....

Uses of Radiation

Q1   The following sentences explain how a smoke detector works, but they are in the wrong order.

Put them in order by labelling them 1 (first) to 6 (last).

☐   The circuit is broken so no current flows.

1   The radioactive source emits alpha particles.

☐   A current flows between the electrodes — the alarm stays off.

☐   The alarm sounds.

☐   The air between the electrodes is ionised by the alpha particles.

☐   A fire starts and smoke particles absorb the alpha radiation.

Q2   The diagram shows how radiation can be used to sterilise surgical instruments.

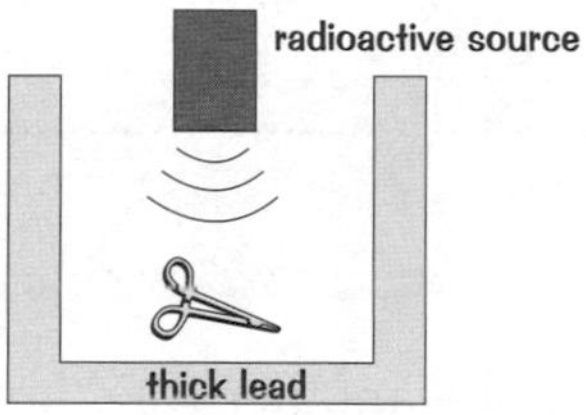

radioactive source

thick lead

a)   What kind of radioactive source is used, and why? In your answer, mention the **type** of radiation emitted (α, β and γ) and the **half-life** of the source.

....

....

b)   What is the purpose of the thick lead?

....

Q3   The table shows the properties of three radioactive isotopes.

a)   Which isotope would be best to use as a medical tracer and why?

....

....

....

Radioactive isotope	Half-life	Type of emission
technetium-99	6 hours	beta/gamma
phosphorus-32	14 days	beta
cobalt-60	5 years	beta/gamma

b)   Which isotope would a hospital use to treat cancer patients? Explain your answer.

....

....

Top Tips: As well as being able to say which radioactive source is the best to use for a particular job, you've also got to be able to say why it's the best. You've got to think about stuff like the type of radiation it emits and what the half-life of the source is. Lots to think about folks.

Radioactivity Safety

Q1 Two scientists are handling samples of radioactive material.

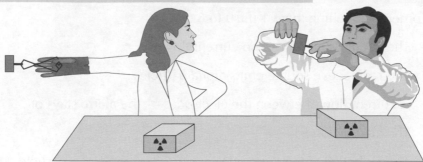

a) One of the scientists is taking sensible safety precautions, but the other is not.
Describe three things which the careless scientist is doing wrong.

1...

2...

3...

b) Describe another way the scientists can reduce their exposure to the radiation,
without using special apparatus or clothing.

....

....

c) How should radioactive samples be stored when they are not in use?

....

Q2 The three different types of radiation can all be dangerous.

a) Which **two** types of radiation can pass through the human body?
Circle the correct answers.

alpha   beta   gamma

b) i) Which type of radiation is usually most dangerous if it's inhaled or swallowed?

....

ii) What effects can this type of radiation have on the human body?

....

....

....

> ## *Top Tips:* You should always handle radioactive sources really carefully. People who work
> with radioisotopes often wear **dosimeters** — badges which record their exposure.

Nuclear Fission and Fusion

Q1 Choose from the following words to complete the passage.

split	chemical	turbine	electricity	uranium-235	water	wine
	steam	moped	generator	reactors	heat	

Inside a nuclear reactor, ... (or plutonium-239) atoms

.... and release .... energy. This energy

is used to turn .... into ....

The steam then turns a ...., which in turn drives a

................................., producing ....

Q2 Explain how a nuclear fission **chain reaction** occurs, starting with a single **plutonium** nucleus absorbing a **slow-moving neutron**.

....

....

....

....

Q3 List four differences between nuclear **fission** and nuclear **fusion**.

1...

2...

3...

4...

Q4 Give two good points and two bad points about **fusion reactors**.

Good points ....

....

Bad points ....

....

The Life Cycle of Stars

Q1 Complete the passage, choosing from the words given below.

gravity	millions	hot	fusion	stable	inwards	outwards	billions	fission	mass

When a protostar gets .... enough, hydrogen nuclei will start to undergo

nuclear .... and the star enters its .... phase (becoming

a main sequence star). The force from the heat generated inside the star (pushing

................................) and the force of gravity (pushing ....) are balanced.

The star might stay in this stable phase for .... of years.

Q2 Stars are formed from clouds of dust and gas.

a) **Why** does the material come together?

....

b) Describe how a **planets** can form around a star.

....

....

Q3 Towards the end of its life, a **main sequence** star will become a **red giant**.

a) What causes a star to become a **red giant**?

....

....

b) Why is a red giant **red**?

....

c) What happens to **small stars** like our Sun after they become red giants?

....

....

Q4 Some red giants start to undergo **more fusion reactions**, glow very brightly and then **explode**. Give the **name** of this explosion, and describe what happens after it.

....

....

....

....

The Life Cycle of Stars

Q5 Below is a diagram showing the **life cycle** of **stars**.

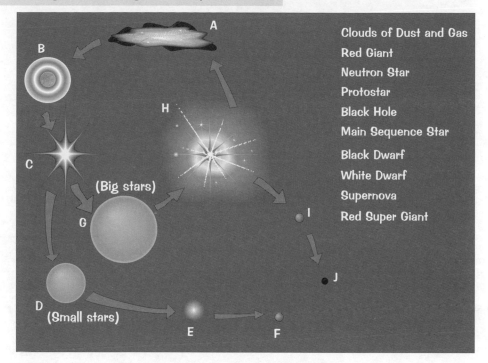

Clouds of Dust and Gas
Red Giant
Neutron Star
Protostar
Black Hole
Main Sequence Star
Black Dwarf
White Dwarf
Supernova
Red Super Giant

Match the letters to the words on the right of the diagram.

A .... B ....

C .... D ....

E .... F ....

G .... H ....

I .... J ....

Q6 The early universe only contained the element **hydrogen**.

a) Why does the universe now contain lots of different elements?

....

b) How are main sequence stars able to maintain their energy output for millions of years?

....

c) Stars form heavy elements such as iron during their stable phases.
Describe how elements **heavier** than iron are created and **spread out** throughout the universe.

....

....

....

....

Mixed Questions — Physics 2b

Q1   The table gives information about four different **radioactive isotopes**.

Source	Type of Radiation	Half-life
radon-222	alpha	3.8 days
technetium-99m	gamma	6 hours
americium-241	alpha	432 years
cobalt-60	beta and gamma	5.27 years

a)   Explain how the atomic structure of cobalt-60 is different from the structure of 'normal' cobalt-59.

....

....

b)   Which sources in the table would be most suitable for each of the uses below?

   medical tracers   **smoke detectors**   **detecting leaks in pipes**

   ....

c)   Radiation can be used to treat cancer.

   i)   What type of radiation is used in this treatment? ....

   ii) Explain why patients often feel very ill while receiving this treatment.

   ....

   ....

d)   Jim measures the count rate of a sample of americium-241 as 120 cpm.
   Roughly how long would it take for the count rate to fall below **4 cpm**? Show your working.

   ....

   ....

e)   Give **two** precautions Jim should take while handling the radioactive sample.

   1. ....

   2. ....

Top Tips: These mixed questions are like a good quality pick 'n' mix — there's a bit of
everything in there: radioactive half-life, stars and electricity... And that's just what the exam'll be like.

Mixed Questions — Physics 2b

Q2 The diagram below shows part of a chain reaction in a nuclear reactor.

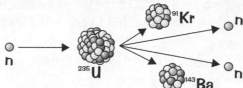

a) What is the name of the type of radioactive decay shown in the diagram? ....

b) This decay happens as part of a chain reaction. Describe what happens in this chain reaction.

....

....

....

c) Describe how thermal energy from the reactor is used to generate electricity.

....

....

Electricity can also be generated using energy released from **nuclear fusion**.

d) Give two advantages of producing electricity using **fusion** rather than the reaction shown above.

1. ....

2. ....

e) Explain why nuclear fusion isn't widely used to generate electricity.

....

....

f) Nuclear fusion is the process by which energy is released in **stars**.

   i) Explain why the universe now contains less hydrogen than it used to.

   ....

   ....

   ii) The **forces** within a star are **balanced** during the **main sequence** period of its life cycle
   Explain the role of **fusion** in this.

   ....

   ....

Mixed Questions — Physics 2b

Q3   Modern electrical appliances are carefully designed to prevent the user getting an electric shock.

a)   Tom's washing machine develops a fault. Part of the live wire touches the metal case.
Explain how the earth wire and fuse work together to prevent Tom getting an electric shock.

....

....

b)   Bob buys a new 'double insulated' television set.

i)   Which wires are in the plug?   ....

ii)   What is meant by 'double insulated'?

....

Q4   Kate charges her mobile phone using a mobile phone charger, rated at 230 V, 600 W.

a)   The battery in the mobile phone supplies a direct current (DC).
Explain what is meant by direct current.

....

b)   Work out whether a 2.5 A, 3 A or 6 A fuse would be best to use in the phone charger.

....

c)   The plastic casing on the plug for Kate's charger has broken.
Explain why Kate shouldn't use the mobile phone charger.

....

....

d)   A mobile phone battery supplies direct current (DC) but mains electricity is alternating current (AC).

The diagram shows a CRO trace from a mains electricity supply on the
island of Bezique. The **timebase** dial was set to 10 ms per large division.

Calculate the **frequency** of Bezique's electricity supply.

....

....

X-rays in Medicine

Q1   In each of the following sentences, circle the correct word(s) from each highlighted pair.

a)   X-rays are **short / long** wavelength electromagnetic
waves that can cause **refraction / ionisation**.

b)   X-rays are **transmitted / absorbed** by healthy soft tissue but are
transmitted / absorbed by dense materials such as bone.

c)   Electronic images can be formed using a **photographic film / charge-coupled device**.

d)   The wavelength of an X-ray is roughly the same as the diameter of a **car / cell / atom**.

Q2   Complete the following paragraph using the words provided.

ill	centre	normal	kill	cells	focused	cancer	rotating

High doses of X-ray radiation will .... living ....

Because of this, X-rays are used to treat .... X-rays are ....

on the tumour using a wide beam. Damage to .... cells can make the

patient feel very .... This damage is minimised by ....

the X-ray beam, keeping the tumour at the ....

Q3   X-ray images can be used to **diagnose** medical conditions.

a)   Describe how X-ray images can be formed using **photographic film**.

....

....

....

....

b)   Briefly describe how X-ray images can be formed **electronically**.

....

....

....

c)   Name one medical condition that X-rays can be used to diagnose.

....

X-rays in Medicine

Q4 Tick the boxes to show whether each of these statements is **true** or **false**.

True **False**

a) The images created using CT scans have a high resolution. ☐ ☐

b) Only soft tissue can be imaged by CT scans. ☐ ☐

c) CT scans use less X-ray radiation than traditional X-ray imaging. ☐ ☐

d) A drawback of CT scanning is its use of ionising radiation. ☐ ☐

Q5 When a CT scan is taken, an image is produced by a computer. Order the statements below 1 to 5 to describe the process of taking a CT scan. The first one has been done for you.

☐ An X-ray tube emits an X-ray beam whilst rotating around the patient.

☐ Multiple slice images are put together to give a three-dimensional picture.

☐ A computer uses the detected X-rays to generate an image of a two-dimensional slice through the body.

☐ Detectors on the opposite side of the scanner measure the intensity of transmitted X-rays.

1 The patient is put inside the CT scanner.

Q6 When radiographers take X-ray 'photographs' or scans of patients, they themselves are exposed to X-rays.

a) Write down **two precautions** radiographers can take to minimise their exposure to X-rays.

1. ....

2. ....

b) Describe **two** ways in which the patient's radiation dose can be **minimised**.

1. ....
   ....

2. ....
   ....

Top Tips: In a CT scan, the image is built up by the subtle differences in different tissues' ability to block the X-ray beam. Because lots of 2D 'slice' images are created, there's no problem of different body parts getting in the way of each other like there is in an X-ray — you get the complete picture.

Ultrasound

Q1 Ultrasound imaging can be used to diagnose soft tissue problems.

   a) What is ultrasound?

....

   b) How can ultrasound of a particular frequency be generated?

....

....

Q2 Ultrasound can be used to detect the existence of a different medium below the surface of an object, and to measure how far below the surface it is.

Sketch a diagram showing what happens when an ultrasound wave hits the boundary between one medium and another.

Q3 A layer of **fat** sitting between a layer of **skin** and a layer of **muscle** is examined using **ultrasound**. The **oscilloscope trace** below shows two pulses of ultrasound from the examination — the first pulse is reflected off the layer of fat and the second is reflected off the layer of muscle. Each **time division** on the oscilloscope represents **5 µs** and the speed of sound through tissue is **1450 m/s**.

   a) Calculate the distance from the ultrasound device to the layer of fat.

$1 µs = 0.000001 s$

....

....

....

   b) Use the oscilloscope trace to calculate the **thickness of the layer of fat**. Give your answer in centimetres and to one decimal place.

....

....

....

Ultrasound Uses

Q1   A concentrated beam of **ultrasound** can be used to treat kidney stones.

a)   What effect does the ultrasound beam have on kidney stones?

....

b)   How are the kidney stone remains removed from the body?

....

c)   Give two reasons why using ultrasound is a good way of treating kidney stones.

1. ....

2. ....

Q2   Doctors use different imaging techniques to diagnose different medical conditions.

a)   Fill in the table below with **one advantage** and **one disadvantage** of ultrasound, X-rays and CT scans.

	Advantage	Disadvantage
Ultrasound imaging		
X-ray photographs		
CT scans		

b)   Which medical imaging technique would you recommend for the planning of complicated brain surgery? Explain your answer

....

....

Q3   Ultrasound can be used in a similar way to **X-rays**.

a)   Why is ultrasound safer than X-rays?

....

b)   State whether X-rays or ultrasound would be used to investigate a suspected broken bone, and explain why.

....

....

....

Refractive Index

Q1   The diagram below shows light entering a glass block.

   a)   As the light enters the glass block it changes direction. What is the name of this effect?

....

   b)   Complete the diagram to show the ray passing through the block
   and emerging from the other side. Include labels A to E for:

A	the refracted ray
B	the emergent ray
C	the normal for the emergent ray
D	the angle of incidence
E	the angle of refraction

normal

incident ray

glass block

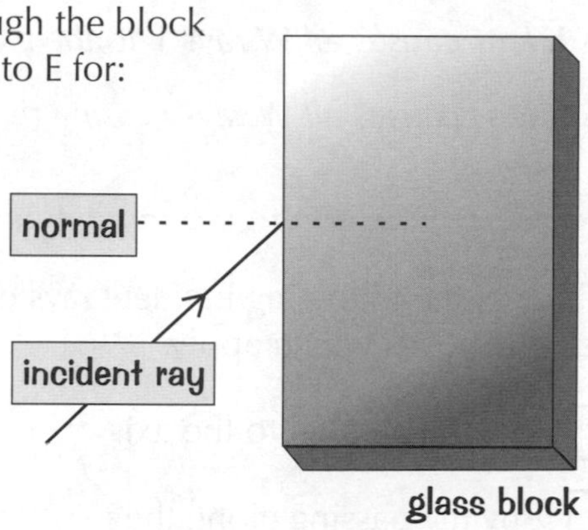

Q2   Every transparent material has a refractive index.

   a)   What is refractive index?

....

   b)   Write down the equation that connects refractive index, angle of incidence and angle of refraction.

....

Q3   A light ray was shone from air into some water. The ray had an **angle of incidence** of **30°**
and an **angle of refraction** of **22°**. Use this data to calculate the **refractive index** of water.

....

....

Q4   The diagram shows light when it refracts from **air**
into **glass**. The refractive index of the glass is 1.514.
Calculate the **angle of refraction** for the incident light.

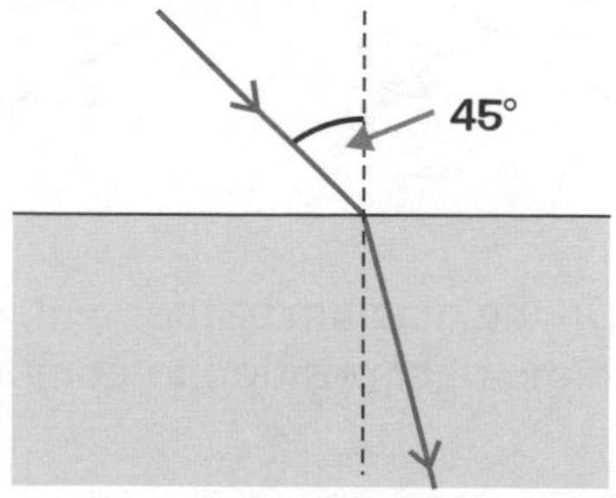

45°

....

....

....

....

Lenses and Images

Q1   Lenses can be either **converging** or **diverging**.

a)   In the following sentences the words **parallel**, **converging**, **principal focus** and **incident** have been replaced by the letters **W**, **X**, **Y**, **Z**. Write down which words are represented by **W**, **X**, **Y** and **Z**.

*An **W** ray passing through the centre of a **X** lens from any angle carries on in the same direction.*

*A **X** lens causes all **W** rays **Y** to the axis to meet at the **Z**.*

*A **X** lens causes all **W** rays passing through the **Z** to emerge **Y** to the axis.*

W .... **X** .... **Y** .... **Z** ....

b)   Which of the following incident rays do not have their direction changed by either type of lens? Tick any boxes which apply.

  ☐ Any ray parallel to the axis   ☐ Any ray passing through the centre of the lens

  ☐ Any ray passing along the axis   ☐ Any ray passing through the principal focus

Q2   Tick the boxes to show whether each of these statements is **true** or **false**.

                                                               True **False**

a)   Only diverging lenses can produce a virtual image.   ☐   ☐

b)   The focal length of a lens is the distance from the centre of the lens to the principal focus.   ☐   ☐

c)   A real image can be projected on a screen   ☐   ☐

d)   A converging lens is concave.   ☐   ☐

Q3   In the ray diagrams below, the pictures of the lenses have been removed.

a)   What type of lens could this be? Underline the correct answer from the options below.

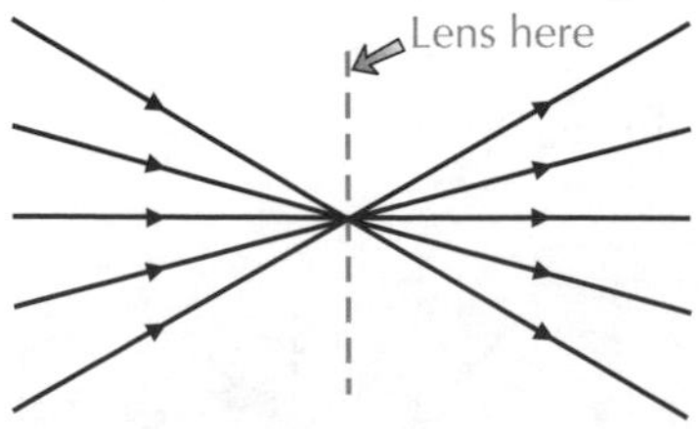

Lens here

    A   A converging lens

    B   A diverging lens

    C   Neither a converging nor a diverging lens

    D   Either a converging or a diverging lens

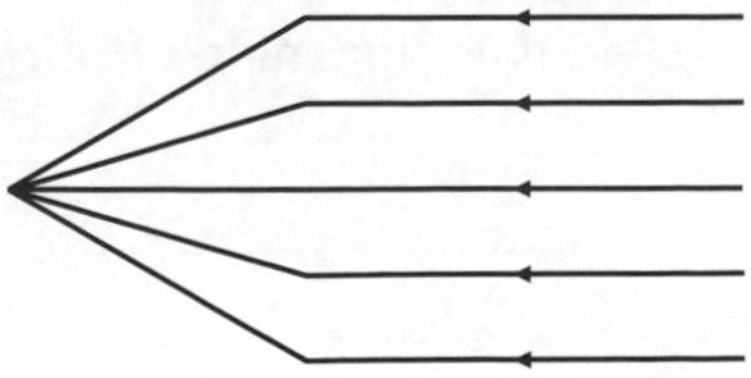

b)   On the diagram to the right, draw a lens of the correct type in the right position to complete the ray diagram.

Top Tips: It may look like we've diverged away from medicine, but fear not, we shall converge on it again in a few pages when we look at what lenses are used for. If you can't guess what I'm talking about, here's a little hint — you almost certainly know someone who wears a pair (and they aren't pants).

Lenses and Images

Q4 Images formed by lenses can either be **real** or **virtual**.

a) What is the difference between a real and a virtual image?

....

....

b) What **three** pieces of information do you need to give to describe the nature of an image?

1. ....

2. ....

3. ....

Q5 This question is about how to **draw ray diagrams** for **converging lenses**.

a) The first step is to draw a ray from the **top** of the object going **parallel** to the **axis** of the lens. Where does this ray pass through when it's refracted?

....

b) The next step is to draw a ray from the top of the object which passes through the lens **without** being refracted. Where does this ray pass through the lens?

....

c) How do the steps above tell you where the **top** of the **image** will be on the ray diagram?

....

Q6 The diagram shows a **diverging lens**.

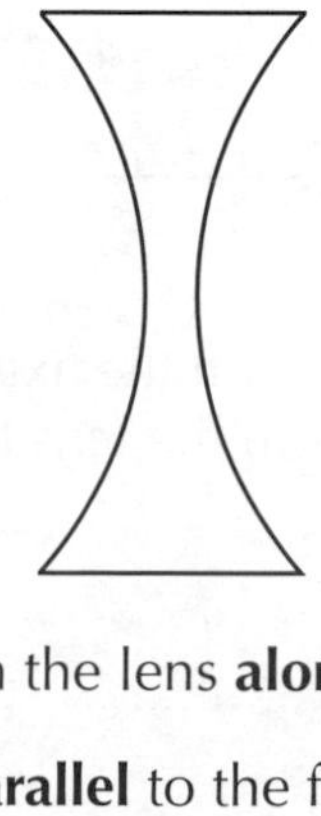

a) Draw the path of a ray passing through the lens **along the axis** from left to right.

b) Draw the paths of two incident rays **parallel** to the first ray, one **above** and one **below** the axis.

c) Sketch in the position of the **virtual principal focus** for the rays shown and label it "F".

Lenses

Q1 Some of this diagram has been hidden. Draw in the rest of the diagram, showing the position of the **object** that produced the image you see.

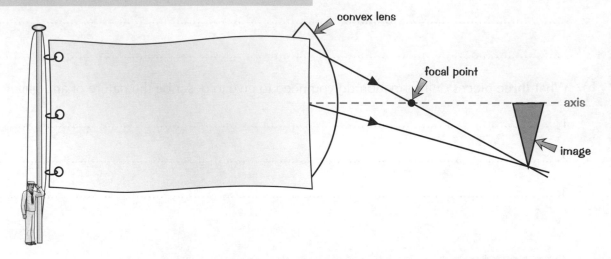

convex lens

focal point

axis

image

Q2 Circle the correct options in this description of images formed by **diverging lenses**.

> Diverging lenses always produce **real / virtual**, **upright / inverted** images which are **smaller / larger** than the object.

Q3 The table below gives information about the images formed by a **converging lens** when the object is at different positions, where F is the principal focus of the lens.

Distance from lens to object	Distance from lens to image	Type of image	Size of image
Greater than 2F	Between 2F and F	Real, inverted	Smaller than object
Equal to 2F		Real, inverted	
Between 2F and F	Greater than 2F		
Less than F	Greater than 2F		Larger than object

a) Fill in the blanks in the table.

b) An object has a height of 1 cm. It stands on the axis of a converging lens, 5 cm away from it. The focal length of the lens (distance from the lens to the principal focus) is 2.5 cm.

   i) What size will the image be?

   ....

   ii) Where will the image be formed, relative to the lens and the object?

   ....

Physics 3a — Medical Applications of Physics

Lenses

Q4 An aubergine is placed **6.1 cm** away from a converging lens with a focal length of **7 cm**.

   a) Will the image formed by the lens be:

      i) upright or inverted? ....

      ii) on the same side of the lens or on the opposite side? ....

      iii) real or virtual? ....

   b) The aubergine is now placed at a distance x from the lens. The image is now bigger than the object and inverted. Which of the options below could be distance x? Circle your answer.

      A 3.9 cm   **B** 7.0 cm   **C** 10.2 cm   **D** 14.0 cm   **E** 15.3 cm

Q5 The diagram below shows an object placed next to a diverging lens. The locations of each principal focus are marked F.

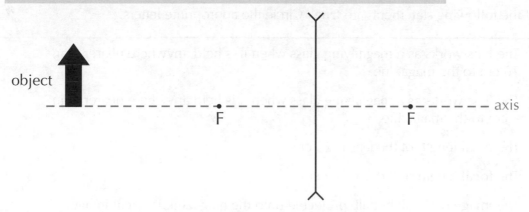

   a) On the diagram, draw the path of a ray coming from the top of the object and travelling in the direction of the centre of the lens.

   b) Draw the path of a ray coming from the top of the object and going towards the principal focus on the far side of the lens.

   c) Draw the image formed by the lens.

Q6 Complete the ray diagram below to show the image produced by the lens.

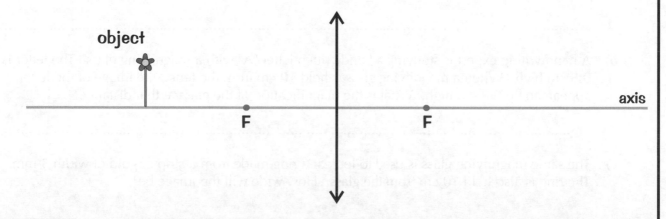

Top Tips: Aubergines aside, you'll be expected to know how to draw lovely ray diagrams for converging and diverging lenses. They can be a bit tricky, but examiners love 'em, so get practising.

Magnification and Power

Q1 Mr Richards is using a **magnifying glass** to read a magazine by the light of an overhead lamp.

a) What sort of lens is used in a magnifying glass?

....

b) Explain why an object you want to view with a magnifying glass must be placed nearer to the lens than the principal focus.

....

....

c) The writing on the magazine is in focus when the lens is a distance of 9 cm or less from the magazine. When the magnifying glass is held exactly 26 cm from the magazine a sharply focused image of the light bulb appears on the magazine.

Three of the following statements are **true**. Circle the appropriate letters.

A	The lens works as a magnifying glass when it is held anywhere nearer than 26 cm to the magazine.
B	The lens works as a magnifying glass when it is held anywhere nearer than 9 cm to the magazine.
C	The focal length of the lens is 26 cm.
D	The focal length of the lens is 9 cm.
E	The image of the light bulb projected onto the magazine is a real image.
F	The image of the light bulb projected onto the magazine is a virtual image.

Q2 The magnification of a magnifying glass depends on the distance of the object from the lens.

a) State the formula for the magnification produced by a lens or mirror.

....

b) A handwriting expert is studying a handwritten letter "A" with a magnifying glass. The letter is 0.5 cm high. When a magnifying glass is held 10 cm from the letter, the image of the letter appears to be 0.8 cm high. What is the magnification of the glass at that distance?

....

c) The same magnifying glass is used to look at a ring made from a strip of gold of width 3 mm. The ring is also held 10 cm from the glass. How wide will the image be?

....

heh
heh
heh...

Magnification and Power

Q3 Convex lenses can also be called **converging lenses**.

a) Which lenses are more powerful? Circle the correct answer.

thinner lenses   *fatter lenses*

b) Write out the equation that relates lens power to focal length.

....

Q4 Dave is using a converging lens to **focus** some parallel rays of light to a point.

a) If the distance between the centre of the lens, X, and the principal focus, Y, is 15 cm, what is the power of the lens?

....

b) Dave wants to increase the distance between the lens and the principal focus, so he switches the lens for one with a power of 5.2 D. Calculate the new distance between X and Y.

....

c) How is the power of a **diverging** lens different to that of a **converging** lens?

....

Q5 Nanny Irene goes to the opticians to get some new glasses.

a) What **two** factors determine the focal length of a lens?

1. ....

2. ....

b) Despite the focal length of her eyes staying the same, Nanny Irene gets new glasses with **thinner** lenses than before. Explain how the manufacturers of her glasses achieved this.

....

....

....

The Eye

Q1 Add labels to complete the diagram of the eye below.

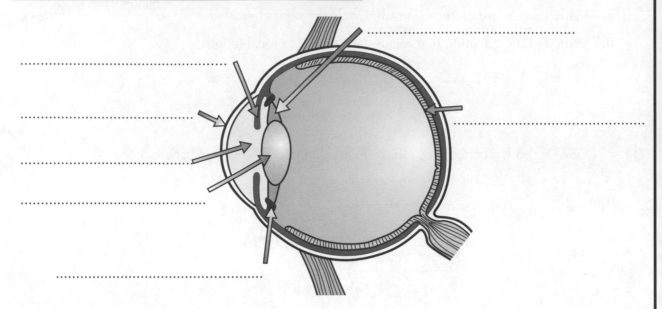

Q2 Tuan is photographing a football match for his school magazine.

a) How is the image produced in a camera similar to the image produced in a human eye?

....

b) Explain why Tuan can't take a picture of an object closer than the focal length of the camera lens.

....

....

c) Circle the correct words or phrases from the alternatives given in the following passage.

For the photograph not to be blurred the image must be formed

at the lens / between the lens and the film / on the film. The image

formed is **smaller / bigger** than the object being photographed because

the object is further than the focal length of the lens. The film

(or CCD) in the camera is the equivalent to the **pupil / retina** in the eye.

Top Tips: Make sure you can label that diagram correctly and have a good understanding of what all the different parts of the eye do — it's the sort of thing that could turn up in an exam all too easily...

Physics 3a — Medical Applications of Physics

The Eye

Q3 **Complete the table** about the functions of different parts of the eye.

Part of the eye	Function
....	Focuses light on the retina
Retina	....
Ciliary muscles	....
....	Hole through which light enters the eye

Q4 Circle the correct word in each pair to complete the passage below.

When you look at distant objects, your ciliary muscles **contract** / **relax**, and pull the lens to make it **thin** / **fat**. The opposite actions happen when you look at near objects. The combined action of the lens and **cornea** / **iris** focuses the light on the **pupil** / **retina** to produce an image. Cells on the **pupil** / **retina** send signals to the brain to be interpreted via the optic nerve.

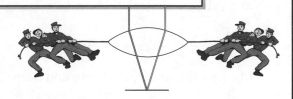

Q5 The range of human eyesight lies between the **near** and **far points**. Complete the definitions of near and far points below.

a) The near point is ....

For normally-sighted adults, the near point is about .... cm.

b) The far point is ....

For normally-sighted adults, the far point is at ....

Correcting Vision

Q1 Common vision problems are caused by the eye focusing an image in the wrong place.

a) Look at the image on the right. Complete the sentences by choosing the correct word(s) from the highlighted options.

The person with this vision defect is **short / long** sighted.

The **near / far** point is closer than infinity, which makes it

difficult to focus on things that are **close up / far away**. The object

in the diagram is brought into focus **in front of / behind** the retina.

object

b) Give **two** possible causes of the problem shown in the diagram.

1. ....

2. ....

c) **i)** Which of the two lenses shown on the right could correct this problem? Circle the correct letter.

A   B

ii) Explain how the lens you chose in part **c)i)** would help to correct the eye problem.

....

....

....

Q2 **Lasers** are increasingly used in surgery.

a) What is a laser?

....

b) Lasers can cut, cauterise and burn tissue.

i) Explain what cauterisation means.

....

ii) Briefly describe how a surgeon can use a laser to correct long or short sight.

....

....

....

Top Tips: Corrective lenses can be in the form of spectacles **or** contact lenses — which ones you wear is up to you. Remember, both can be either diverging or converging lenses. Good 'ol lenses.

Total Internal Reflection

Q1 Doctors can use an **endoscope**, a thin tube containing **optical fibres**, to look inside a patient's body.

a) What type of radiation is sent along optical fibres?

....

b) What material could the optical fibres in the endoscope be made from?

....

c) Explain why endoscopes contain two bundles of optical fibres.

....

....

d) Optical fibres work because of repeated **total internal reflections**.
Complete the ray diagrams below. The critical angle for glass/air is 42°.

You'll need to measure the angle of incidence for each one — carefully.

Q2 Martin wants to buy a ring for Marion. He compares a **diamond** ring with a **glass** imitation ring.

a) The critical angle between glass and air is **42°**. Calculate the refractive index of glass.

....

b) Martin knows that the refractive index of diamond is **2.4**.
Calculate the critical angle between diamond and air.

....

c) The glass imitation ring is cut in exactly the same way as the diamond ring.
Which of the two rings will be the most **sparkly**?
Explain your answer using your answers from parts **a)** and **b)**.

Think about how much light will be reflected.

....

....

....

....

Mixed Questions — Physics 3a

Q1   Lara is having a great time investigating how light travels through media.

a) Lara shines a ray of light passing across the **boundary** between two media.

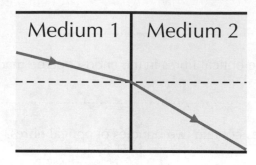

i) Which of Medium 1 and Medium 2 is air and which is glass?

Medium 1 is ....   **Medium 2 is** ....

ii) Explain your answer to **a) i)**. ....

....

....

b) **i)** In which of these situations could Lara get total internal reflection? Circle the correct letter(s).

    A Light is travelling from air into water.
    B Light is travelling from glass into air.

ii) Explain your answer to **b) i)**. ....

....

....

c) Lara investigates refraction of light in water by shining a beam of light **up** through a fish tank to the air above. She finds the **critical angle** of light travelling from water into air is **49°**.

i) Calculate the refractive index of water.

....

....

ii) She shines the beam of light down into the water from the air at an angle of 20°.
Use your answer from part **c) i)** to calculate the angle of refraction of the light.

....

....

....

Mixed Questions — Physics 3a

Q2   Andrew and Cassie are looking at a shell.
They can see it because images **form on their retinas**.

a)   Complete the paths of the light rays on the diagram below so that
the image of the shell is correctly brought into focus on the retina.

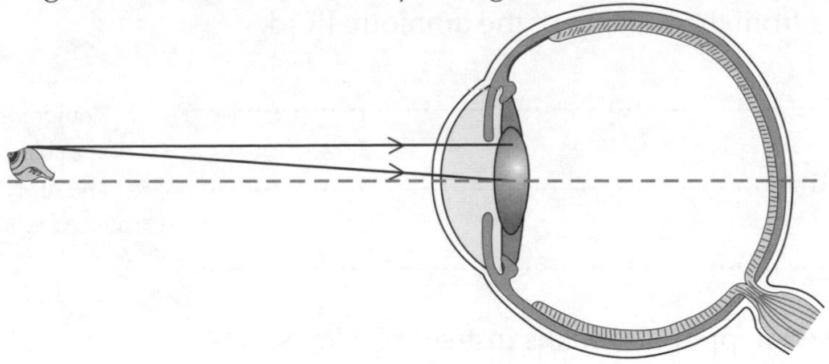

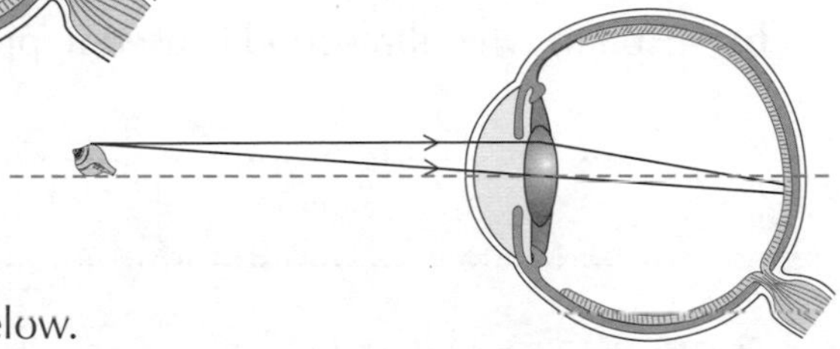

b)   The light entering Cassie's eye is shown in the
diagram to the right. Her lens is working correctly.

Circle the correct words to complete the sentences below.

> Cassie's eyeball is too **long / short,** so images form **behind / in front of** her retina.
>
> This can be corrected by **concave / convex** spectacle lenses as these make light rays converge.

c)   Cassie wears glasses to correct her vision.
The lens for her right eye has a focal length of **0.4 m**.

   i) Calculate the **power** of the lens.

   ....

   ii) The lens for her left eye is made of the **same material** as the lens for her right eye,
   but has a **higher power**. Describe how the two lenses will differ in appearance.

   ....

d)   Andrew uses a **magnifying glass** to examine the shell, which is **1.8 cm** tall.
He finds that to magnify the shell, he must hold the lens less than **3 cm** from it.
When he holds the magnifying glass **2.5 cm** away from the shell, the image formed is **4 cm** tall.

   i) What is the focal length of this lens?

   ....

   ii) What is the magnification of the lens at 2.5 cm?

   ....

   iii) Is the image real or virtual? Explain your answer.

   ....

   ....

Mixed Questions — Physics 3a

Q3   **Ultrasound imaging** is a valuable technique in many different medical investigations.

a)   A pulse of ultrasound is directed toward an unborn fetus. It **partially reflects** when it reaches the amniotic fluid and again when it reaches the body of the fetus. An oscilloscope trace shows that the time between the reflected pulses is **26 µs**. The speed of sound through the fluid is 1500 m/s. Calculate how far the fetus is from the outside of the amniotic fluid.

....

....

....

Remember — when something is reflected, the distance it has travelled is there and back.

b)   Explain why ultrasound is used in pre-natal scans instead of X-rays.

....

....

c)   X-rays can be used to treat cancer, but ultrasound can't. Explain why.

....

....

d)   CT scans can produce very clear images of inside the body, but doctors always try to keep their use to an absolute minimum. Explain why doctors will only take CT scans when it is absolutely necessary.

....

....

e)   Describe the process of producing a **three-dimensional CT image**. Include the words in the box below in your answer.

X-ray tube	slice	detectors	rotated	computer

....

....

....

....

....

Top Tips: Examiners love to ask questions that get you to show that you really know what you're talking about — and a good example is getting you to compare the different medical imaging processes. Make sure you are totally clued up on the pros and cons of X-rays, ultrasound and CT scans.

Turning Forces and the Centre of Mass

Q1 a) Fill in the blanks in the following passage, using the words supplied.

pivot	perpendicular	moment	force

The turning effect of a .... is called its ....

It can be found by multiplying the force by the .... distance from

the line of action of the force to the ....

b) What are the units in which moments are measured? ....

Q2 To open a door, its handle needs to be **rotated clockwise**.

a) A force of 45 N is exerted vertically downwards on the door-handle at a distance of 0.1 m from the pivot. What is the **moment** of the force?

....

b) Pictures **A**, **B**, **C** and **D** show equal forces being exerted on the handle.

  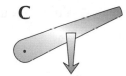

Which of the forces shown (**A**, **B**, **C** or **D**) exerts:

i) the largest moment? ....   **ii)** the smallest moment? ....

Q3 A baby's pram toy consists of a toy banana hanging from a bar over the pram.

a) The banana is hanging **at rest**, as shown.
Draw a line on which the centre of mass **must** fall.

b) Complete the following sentences by choosing from the words and phrases below:

level with	vertically below	perpendicular	moment	centre of mass	horizontal

When a suspended object's .... is ....

the pivot, the .... distance between the line of action of the

gravitational force and the pivot is zero. This means that there is no

.... due to the object's weight.

Turning Forces and the Centre of Mass

Q4 You can think of the **centre of mass** as the point where all the mass of an object seems to be concentrated.

a) Using lines of symmetry, find the centre of mass of each of these shapes:

b) **Circle** the correct answer to complete this sentence. The centre of mass of a raindrop is:

A at the top **D** near the bottom

B near the top **E** at the bottom

C midway down

Q5 Two men, one at each end, hold a 0.8 m long metal pole weighing 130 N so that it is in a **horizontal** position. One man accidentally lets go of his end.

What is the moment on the pole due to its weight an instant after he lets go?

Draw a diagram.

First, find the centre of mass of the pole.

....

....

....

Q6 Some pupils want to find the centre of mass of an **irregularly shaped** piece of cardboard. They are equipped with a stand to hang the card from, a plumb line and a pencil. They make a hole near one edge of the card and hang it from the stand.

a) What steps should they take next in order to find the centre of mass?

....

....

....

....

b) How could they make their result more reliable?

....

....

Balanced Moments and Levers

Q1   A 2 N weight (Weight A) sits 20 cm to the left of the pivot of a balance.
A 5 N weight (Weight B) is placed 16 cm to the left of the pivot.

a)   What is the moment exerted by **Weight A**? ....

b)   What is the moment exerted by **Weight B**? ....

c)   How far to the right of the pivot should Weight C (8 N) be placed to **balance** A and B?

....

....

d)   If all three of the weights were exactly **twice as far** away from the pivot,
would the balance tip over to one side?   Explain your answer.

....

Q2   Barbara uses a wheelbarrow to move things around her allotment.
She says "I love my wheelbarrow.   It makes it so much easier to lift everything."

Explain **how** a wheelbarrow reduces the
amount of force needed to lift an object.

Hint: a wheelbarrow is
just a type of lever.

....

....

....

....

....

Q3   One side of a drop-leaf table is pivoted on a hinge
and supported 5 cm from its edge by a table leg.
The table leaf is 80 cm long and weighs 40 N.

Find the force, F, exerted by the table leg (when the
table leaf is fully extended).

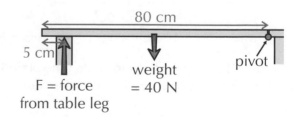

....

....

....

Moments, Stability and Pendulums

Q1 The top drawer of a two-drawer filing cabinet is full of heavy files, but the bottom drawer is empty.

Why is the cabinet in danger of falling over if the top drawer is fully pulled out?

....

....

....

aaaaaarghhhh

Q2 The pictures show three different designs for **vases**.

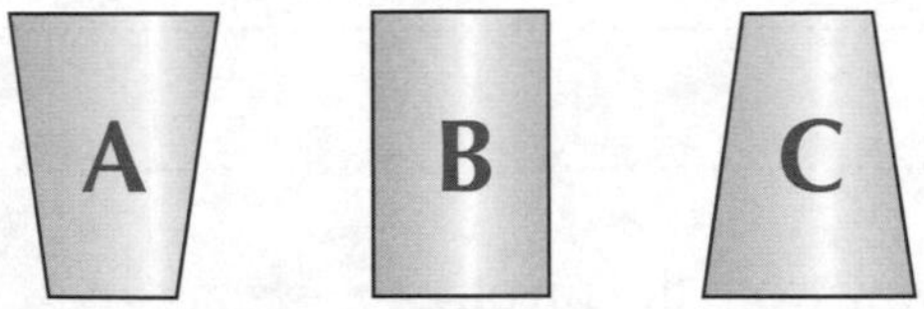

A   B   C

Which vase will be **most stable**? Explain your answer.

....

....

Q3 The diagram to the right shows a cart being used to carry coal along a slope. The centre of mass of the cart, when full, is shown.

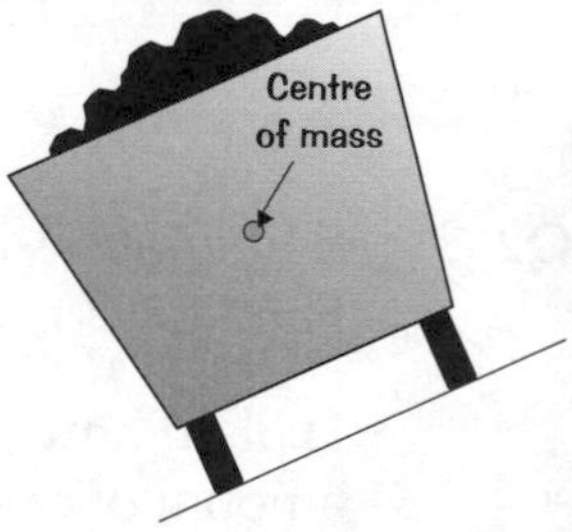

Centre of mass

a) Explain why the cart **doesn't** topple over when on the slope.

....

....

b) Suggest **one** way in which the stability of the cart could be improved.

....

Q4 A magician is using a pendulum to practise hypnotism.
The pendulum swings with a time period of 1.25 s.

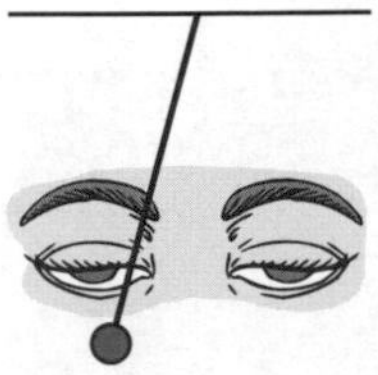

a) Calculate the frequency of the pendulum.

....

....

b) The magician decides the time period of the pendulum's swing needs to be longer to work best. Suggest **one** way in which he could increase the time period of the pendulum.

....

Top Tips: In the exam, you might be expected to look at an object and describe how its design affects its stability. You're always looking for the same sort of things though — where its centre of mass is and how wide its base is. My massive bottom means I'm fairly stable and very difficult to topple.

Physics 3b — Forces and Electromagnetism

Hydraulics

Q1 Fill in the blanks in the following passage, using the words supplied.

transmitted	force	equally	incompressible	pressure	flow

Liquids can .... and are virtually .... These

properties mean that a .... exerted at one point on a liquid will be

.... to other points in the liquid. .... can also

be transmitted through a liquid — it is transmitted .... in all directions.

Q2 The diagram on the right shows a **simple hydraulic system**.

a) Hydraulic systems are used as '**force multipliers**'.
Briefly describe how a hydraulic system works as a 'force multiplier'.

....

....

....

....

b) A force of 650 N is applied to the 1st piston, which has a cross-sectional area of 0.0025 m^2.

i) Calculate the pressure created in the liquid by the first piston.

....

ii) What will the pressure of the liquid at the 2nd piston be? Explain your answer.

....

....

Q3 The diagram below shows two syringes connected by a tube. The entire system is filled with water.
When a **force** is applied to one syringe, water passes through the tube to the other syringe.

A force of 18 N is applied to the piston of the small syringe.

a) Calculate the pressure created by the force.

....

....

b) Calculate the force acting on the piston of the larger syringe.

....

....

Circular Motion

Q1 Which of the following is the **best explanation** of acceleration? Circle the appropriate letter.

    A   an increase in speed   **D**   a change in velocity

    B   a change in direction   **E**   a change in speed

    C   an increase in velocity

Q2 The diagram below shows a clock with hands that move **steadily** around the clock-face.

  a) Draw and label with 'A' an arrow on the diagram to show the direction of the **velocity** of the tip of the **minute hand**.

  b) Draw and label with 'B' an arrow to show the direction of the **acceleration** of the tip of the **hour hand**.

Q3 A **satellite** orbiting the Earth travels at a constant speed.

  a) Is the satellite accelerating? Explain your answer.

    ....

  b) Put a tick next to each true statement below.

    ☐   "If a body is accelerating then there must be a resultant force acting on it."

    ☐   "The forces acting on a body going round in a circle at a steady speed must be balanced."

    ☐   "If there is no resultant force acting on a body then it carries on moving in a straight line at the same speed."

  c) What is the general name for a force that keeps a body moving in a circular path?

    ....

  d) Draw lines to match up the following bodies with the force that keeps them moving in a circle.

A runner running round a circular track	Gravity
A satellite in orbit round the Earth	Tension
The seats at the ends of the spokes of a spinning fairground ride	Friction

Q4 Circle the correct options in these sentences.

  a) The greater the mass of a body, the **smaller / greater** the force needed to keep it moving in a circle.

  b) The faster the speed of a body, the **smaller / greater** the force needed to keep it moving in a circle.

  c) A cyclist rides round a circular track at a speed of 20 m/s. The frictional force between his tyres and the track is 1467 N. He speeds up to 21 m/s — the frictional force changes to **1617 N / 1331 N**.

Magnetic Fields

Q1 Which **one** of the following statements is correct? Tick the box next to the correct statement.

☐ Magnetic fields can only be detected by another magnetic device such as a compass.

☐ Items made from iron, aluminium and steel are all attracted to a magnet.

☐ Magnetic fields can exert a force on a wire carrying a current.

☐ The magnetic field created around a current-carrying wire points in the same direction as the flow of current through the wire.

Q2 The diagram below shows a wire carrying a current passing through a piece of flat card.

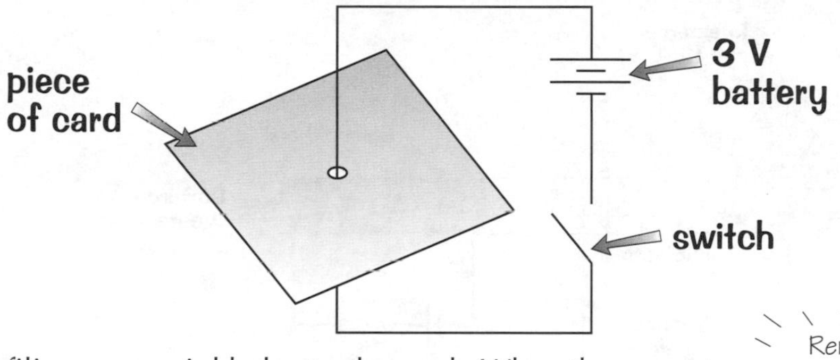

piece of card

3 V battery

switch

Some iron filings are sprinkled onto the card. When the current is switched on, a pattern develops in the iron filings.

Remember the direction of conventional current flow. Then use the Right-Hand Thumb Rule.

On the diagram, sketch the pattern which the iron filings make, including arrows to show the direction of the magnetic field.

Q3 The diagram below shows a coil of wire (a solenoid) carrying a current.

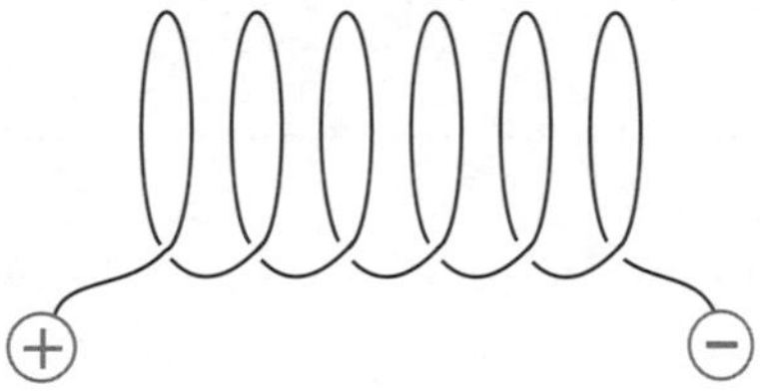

$+$ $-$

a) Draw the shape of the magnetic field around the coil.

b) What effect would the solenoid have on a piece of soft iron placed near one of its ends?

....

....

c) A soft iron core is placed in the middle of the coil. The core becomes magnetised when a current flows through the wire, and loses its magnetism when the current is switched off.

What is the name of this type of magnet?

....

Magnetic Fields

Q4   Electromagnets are often found in cranes used for lifting iron and steel.
Explain why electromagnets are **more useful** than ordinary magnets for this purpose.

....

....

....

Q5   The diagram shows how a solenoid can be used as a relay to switch an external circuit on and off.

To external
circuit (230 V)

Solenoid coil

Soft iron
core

Metal
contacts

Springy
metal

Low voltage
DC source

Switch

To external
circuit (230 V)

a)   Describe what happens when the switch is closed and then opened again.

....

....

....

....

b)   Give two reasons why a **soft iron** core is used in the solenoid.

....

....

....

....

Top Tips: Only **iron**, **steel** (which contains iron), **nickel** and **cobalt** are magnetic. Other metals won't stick to magnets. That's why you sometimes get magnets next to aluminium recycling bins — if a can sticks to the magnet, you know it's **not** aluminium.

Physics 3b — Forces and Electromagnetism

The Motor Effect

Q1 Complete the passage below using the words supplied.

force	angle	stronger	current	magnetic field	motor	permanent magnets

A wire carrying an electric current has a .... around it. This

can interact with the magnetic fields of other wires or of ....

to produce a .... and sometimes movement. A bigger .... or a

.... magnet will produce a bigger force. The size of the force will also depend on

the .... at which the two magnetic fields meet each other. A force is experienced

by a current-carrying wire in a magnetic field — this is known as the .... effect.

Q2 The diagram shows an electrical wire between two magnetic poles. When the current is switched on, the wire moves at right angles to the magnetic field.

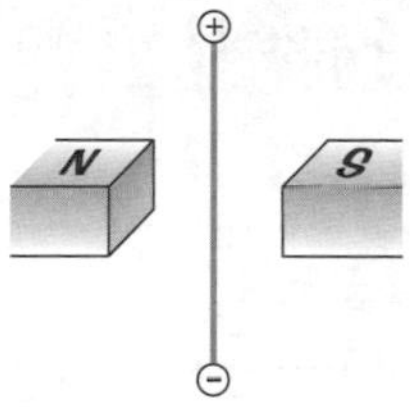

a) Using Fleming's Left-Hand Rule, state which way the wire will move.

....

b) How could the wire be made to move in the opposite direction?

....

Q3 Read the three statements below. Tick the box next to each statement that you think is **true**.

☐ A current-carrying wire will not experience a force if it is parallel to the magnetic field of a permanent magnet.

☐ A current-carrying wire will not experience a force if it is at right-angles to the magnetic field of a permanent magnet.

☐ A current-carrying wire will not experience a force if it is at an angle of 45° to the magnetic field of a permanent magnet.

Q4 The diagram shows an aerial view of a copper wire carrying a current down into the page.

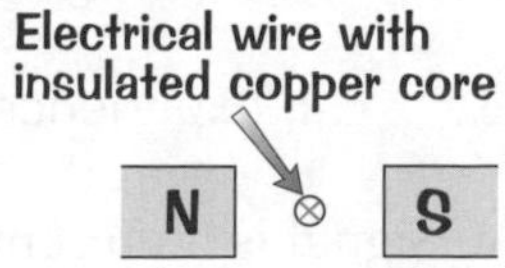

Electrical wire with insulated copper core

N ⊗ S

State which way the wire will move.

....

The Simple Electric Motor

Q1   Which of the following will **not** make an electric motor spin faster? Tick **one** of the boxes.

☐   Using a stronger magnetic field.

☐   Using a bigger current.

☐   Using a commutator.

Q2   Read the three statements below. Tick the box next to each statement that you think is **true**.

☐   The split-ring commutator increases the size of the electric current.

☐   The split-ring commutator reverses the direction of the current every half turn by swapping the contacts to the DC supply.

☐   The split-ring commutator makes the motor rotate in a different direction.

Q3   Suggest two ways in which the direction of spin of a simple DC motor can be reversed.

....

....

Q4   The electric motor is often used in lifts in tall buildings and mines.
Describe briefly how an electric motor can be used to raise (and lower) a lift cage.

....

....

....

Q5   Fill in the blanks, using the words below, to explain how a **loudspeaker** works. Use the **diagram** of a loudspeaker to the right to help you.

| move | amplifier | force | field |
| sound | magnetic | frequency | current |

The loudspeaker relies on the fact that a wire carrying a .... in a

.... can experience a .... A coil is attached

to a cardboard or plastic cone. An AC signal is then sent to the coil from an ....

This makes the coil .... and causes the cone to vibrate. The cone vibrates at the

same .... as the signal from the amplifier and produces ....

Electromagnetic Induction

Q1 The apparatus in the diagram below can be used to demonstrate electromagnetic induction.

Centre-reading ammeter

N   S

Electrical wire

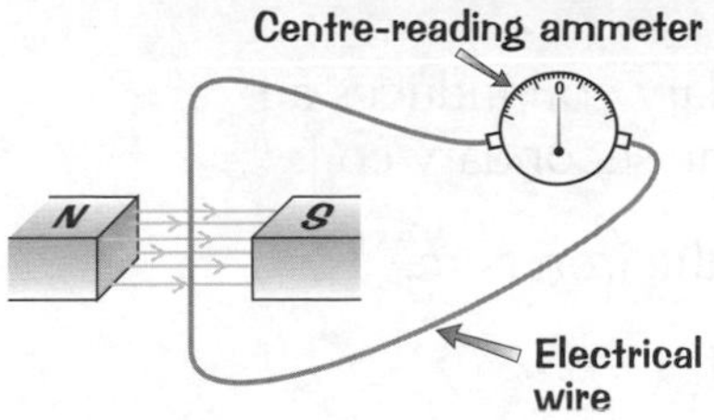

a) What is electromagnetic induction?

....

....

....

b) Describe how you could use the apparatus to demonstrate electromagnetic induction.

....

....

c) What would you see on the ammeter?

....

d) What effect would swapping the magnets have?

....

Q2 Moving a magnet inside an electric coil produces a trace on a cathode ray oscilloscope.

When the magnet was pushed **inside** the coil, **trace A** was produced on the screen.

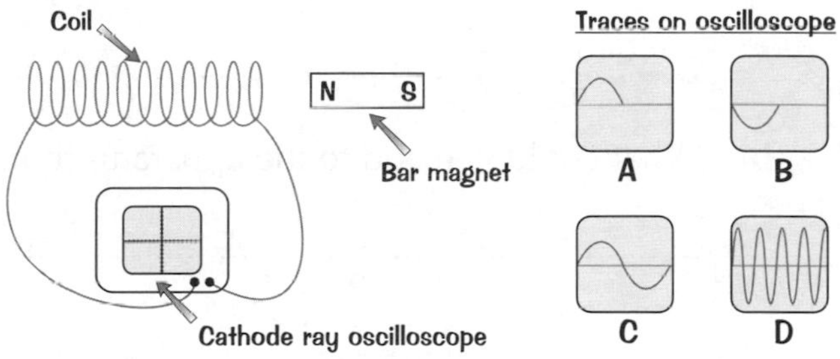

Coil

N   S

Bar magnet

Cathode ray oscilloscope

Traces on oscilloscope

A   B   C   D

a) Explain how trace B could be produced.

....

....

b) Explain how trace C could be produced.

....

c) Explain how trace D could be produced.

....

Q3 To the right is a diagram of a **dynamo** used to power lights on a bicycle. Use the diagram to help you explain **how** a dynamo works.

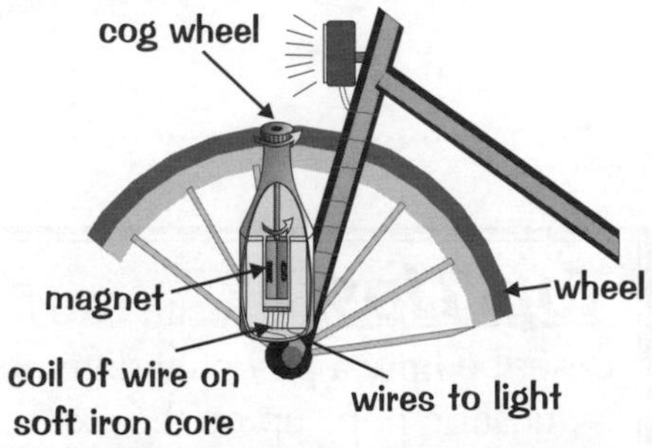

cog wheel

magnet

coil of wire on soft iron core

wheel

wires to light

....

....

....

....

Transformers

Q1 The sentences below describe how a **transformer** works but are in the wrong order. Number the boxes 1 to 5 to show the correct order.

☐ The magnetic field produced inside the secondary coil induces an alternating potential difference at the ends of the secondary coil.

☐ This produces an alternating magnetic field in the iron core.

☐ An alternating current flows in the primary coil.

☐ If this is applied to an external circuit, an alternating current will flow in that circuit.

☐ A source of alternating potential difference is applied to the primary coil.

Q2 Look at the diagram to the right showing two electrical circuits.

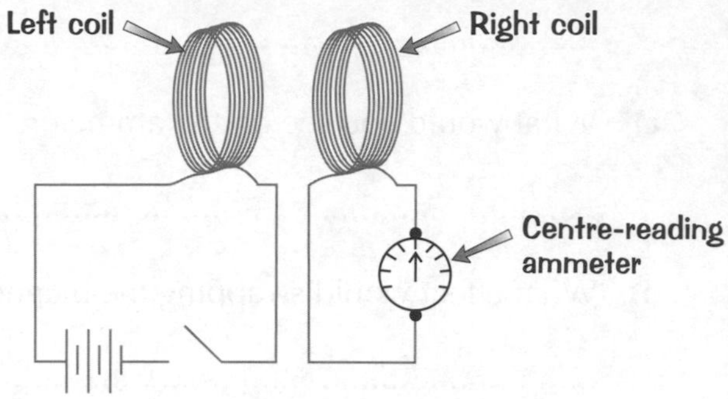

When the switch is closed, a deflection is seen on the ammeter and then the needle returns to zero. When the switch is opened again, a deflection is seen in the opposite direction.

Left coil

Right coil

Centre-reading ammeter

a) Explain why this happens.

....

....

....

b) What could you add to the apparatus to make the needle move further?

....

Q3 Tick the boxes to indicate whether the following statements are **true** or **false**.

	True	False
Step-down transformers have fewer turns on the secondary coil than the primary coil.	☐	☐
If you put a DC into the primary coil, a DC will be produced in the secondary coil.	☐	☐
When a transformer is operating it behaves as though a bar magnet was being pushed into and pulled out of the secondary coil.	☐	☐

Q4 Many household electrical goods such as computers and radios need a lower voltage than the 230 V mains voltage. What sort of transformer is used to reduce the voltage for these goods?

....

Top Tips: It can be a bit tricky remembering how a transformer works — make sure you can describe **how** a potential difference is induced in the **secondary coil**. Not only will it be useful in case a question pops up on the exam, but it's also a great icebreaker topic when meeting new people.

Transformers

Q5   The following statements are **false**. Below each statement, write a correct version.

a)   A transformer consists of an iron core and one wire coil.

....

b)   Step-up transformers have more turns on the primary coil than the secondary coil.

....

....

c)   In a step-down transformer the potential difference across the secondary coil is greater than the potential difference across the primary coil.

....

....

....

Q6   Transformers have an **iron core**.

Derek's transformation didn't go quite as he'd planned.

a)   Explain why a potential difference is induced in the **secondary coil** when an alternating current flows in the primary coil.

....

....

b)   Why do transformers work with **alternating** current **only**?

....

....

Q7   Ash is discussing transformers with his friends. He says:

> "The core of a transformer has to be made of a conducting material such as iron so the current can get through."

Is Ash right or wrong? Give a reason for your answer.

Ash is .... because ....

....

Physics 3b — Forces and Electromagnetism

Transformers

Q8 Many modern appliances use **switch mode transformers**.

a) Tick the boxes to show whether the following statements
about switch mode transformers are **true** or **false**.

	True	False
They usually operate at a frequency between 50 kHz and 200 kHz.	☐	☐
They're usually smaller and lighter than traditional transformers.	☐	☐
They operate at lower frequencies than traditional transformers.	☐	☐
They use very little power when they're switched on and no load is applied.	☐	☐

b) Name **one** device that uses a switch mode transformer.

....

Q9 Tim is investigating a transformer. He uses it to power a **spotlight**, and measures
the **voltage** and **current** for both the **primary** and **secondary coils**. Here are his results.

Voltage to primary coil (V)	Current in primary coil (A)	Voltage to secondary coil (V)	Current in secondary coil (A)
240	0.25	12	5.0

a) Is Tim's transformer a **step-up** or **step-down** transformer? Give a reason for your answer.

....

....

b) i) Calculate the power in the **primary** coil when using the spotlight.

....

....

ii) Calculate the power in the **secondary** coil when using the spotlight.

....

....

c) What idea about the **efficiency** of a transformer is confirmed by Tim's results?

....

___

> ## Top Tips:
> Crikey, you should know transformers inside and out after all those wonderful
> questions... and there's another juicy page of questions still to come. Make sure you can rearrange
> the transformer equations with ease and know the advantages of switch mode transformers too.

Transformers

Q10 A transformer has 100 turns in its primary coil and 4000 turns in its secondary coil. What input voltage would produce an output voltage of 10 000 V?

....

....

Q11 Use the **transformer equation** to complete the following table.

Number of turns on primary coil	Voltage to primary coil (V)	Number of turns on secondary coil	Voltage to secondary coil (V)
1000	12	4000	
1000		2000	20
1000	12		12
	33 000	500	230

Q12 A transformer has **5000** turns on its **primary** coil and **8000** turns on its **secondary** coil.

a) If the input voltage is 230 V, find the output voltage.

....

b) Andy has built a radio which needs a 20 V electricity supply. The mains supply to Andy's house is 230 V. How could Andy adapt the transformer described above to make it suitable for his radio?

....

....

....

....

Q13 A transformer in an adaptor is used to **step down** a **230 V** mains electricity supply to the **110 V** needed for an electric fan heater.

Calculate the current drawn by the transformer from the mains supply, if the current through the heater is **20 A**. Assume that the transformer is 100% efficient.

....

....

<u>Mixed Questions — Physics 3b</u>

Q1   Point P marks the pivot point on the wheelbarrow.

a) Take moments about P to find the **vertical** force, F, that needs to be applied to the handles of the wheelbarrow to just lift it off the ground.

....

....

b) The wheelbarrow tipped over while it was being pushed, fully loaded, across some rocky ground. Explain why this happened using the phrases **resultant moment** and **centre of mass** in your answer.

....

....

c) Write down **two** factors which affect the stability of an object.

1. ....

2. ....

Q2   Mick takes his younger brother Huck on a trip to a fairground.

a) They decide to go on the swinging pirate ship first. If the time period of each swing of the ship is **2 seconds**, calculate the **frequency** of the ship.

....

b) Mick wins a goldfish on a fairground stall. When he squeezes the top of bag, water squirts out of a hole at the bottom. Explain briefly, in terms of **forces**, why this happens.

....

....

c) Mick decides to try out the "Test Your Strength!" game.

The game works using a **simple hydraulic system** (see right). Mick uses a wooden mallet to hit a small piston.

Use the diagram to explain why the **upwards** force at the larger piston will be **greater** than the force of the mallet on the smaller piston.

....

....

....

Physics 3b — Forces and Electromagnetism

Mixed Questions — Physics 3b

Q3   The diagram below shows how an **electromagnet** can be used to switch on a car's starter motor.

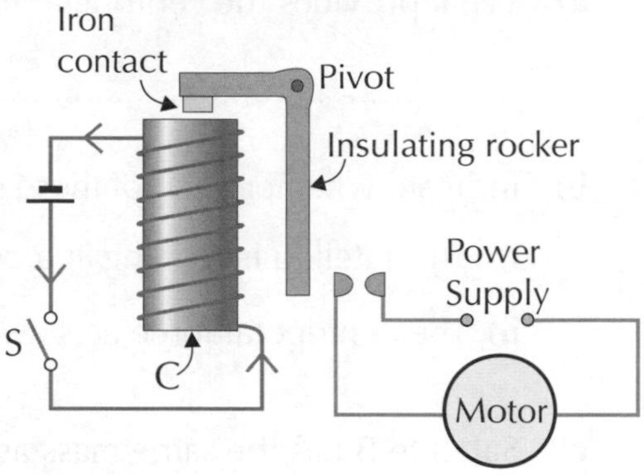

a)   What is the function of the iron core, C?

....

....

b)   Describe what happens when the switch, S, is closed.

....

....

....

....

Q4   The diagram below shows a simple **motor**. The coil is rotating as shown.

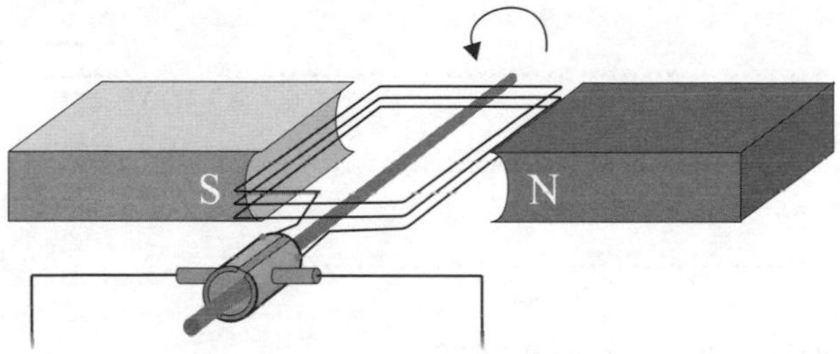

a)   On the diagram, draw arrows labelled 'F' to show the direction of the **force** on each arm of the coil.

b)   Draw arrows labelled 'I' on each arm of the coil to show the direction the **current** is flowing.

c)   State two ways of increasing the **speed** of this motor.

1...

2...

Q5   The diagram shows a **bicycle dynamo**.

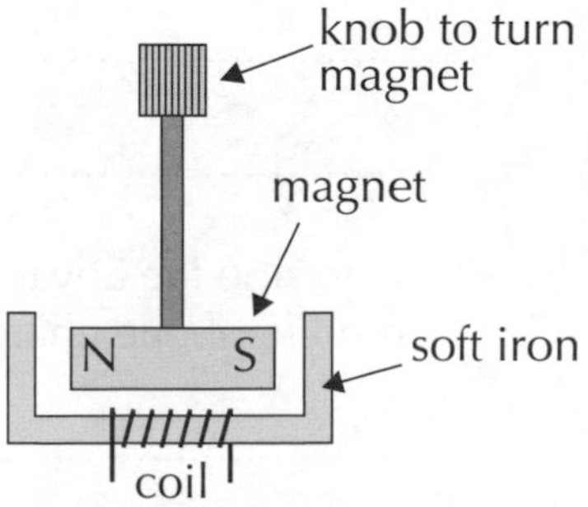

a)   What happens in the coil of wire when the knob is rotated **clockwise** at a constant speed? Explain your answer.

....

....

....

b)   What would change if the magnet were rotated **anticlockwise** (at the same speed as before)?

....

Mixed Questions — Physics 3b

Q6 TV satellite **A** shown below orbits the Earth at a distance of 35 800 km above the surface.

a) What provides the centripetal force that keeps the satellite moving in a circular path?

....

b) Indicate whether each of these statements is true or false.

	True	False
i) The satellite is moving at a constant velocity.	☐	☐
ii) The centripetal force acts away from the centre of the circle.	☐	☐

c) Satellite B has the same mass as satellite A and is in orbit 40 000 km above the Earth.

Which satellite, A or B, has the greatest centripetal force acting on it? ....

Q7 The diagram shows a traditional **transformer**.

a) What is the output voltage, V?

....

....

....

230 V AC — 1000 turns — 200 turns — (V)

b) Transformers are usually wound on a **core**.

i) Name the metal used for the core of the transformer. ....

ii) Why is the core a necessary part of a transformer?

....

....

c) A different transformer is needed to 'step down' a power supply from 33 kV to 230 V.
It has 2000 turns on its primary coil. How many turns should it have on its secondary coil?

....

....

d) Describe the advantages of using a **switch mode transformer** in a
mobile phone charger, compared to a traditional transformer.

....

....

....